SMILE TO
YOUR HEART
MEDITATIONS

SMILE TO
YOUR HEART
MEDITATIONS

Simple Practices for Peace, Health and Spiritual Growth

IRMANSYAH EFFENDI, M.Sc.

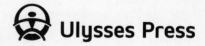 **Ulysses Press**

Published in the United States by
ULYSSES PRESS
P.O. Box 3440
Berkeley, CA 94703
www.ulyssespress.com

ISBN13: 978-1-56975-815-1
Library of Congress Catalog Number: 2010925865

Printed in the United States by Bang Printing

10 9 8 7 6 5 4 3 2 1

Acquisitions: Kelly Reed
Managing Editor: Claire Chun
Editor: Richard Harris
Editorial/Production: Lauren Harrison, Judith Metzener
Front cover design: what!design @ whatweb.com
Cover artwork: © istockphoto.com/Elena Ray

May all beings open their hearts more to the Creator,
True Source

CONTENTS

INTRODUCTION

We are meant to be happy.

If you look at the motivations behind our thoughts and actions—conscious and unconscious—they're all to get us closer to the feeling, or at least the idea, of happiness.

Yet in spite of our worldly successes and social relationships, we sometimes feel lonely, empty, as if something is missing. Even when we experience happiness, it tends to be more of a brief touch than a lasting embrace. We seem to slip back to a lower plane, a place of wanting, again and again.

Psychologists, economists, poets—and, most importantly, you—have long asked why. But, for all of the scholarship and human insight across the centuries, nobody has found a complete and enduring answer. Perhaps because it's been too close to see...

The answer, the truth, is our heart. Not the physical heart that beats in our chest, but our spiritual heart: the key connection to True Source, the Source of peace, calmness, and joy. In

9

opening and using our heart, we're blessed with a lasting peace and happiness that we can feel—actually and really feel—as we go about our daily lives. (Because opening our heart is universal and applies to all religions and faiths, please feel free to replace the term "True Source" with whatever name you use to refer to the Source of Light and Love). It is my joy to share with you in this book not only information about the heart but also simple and effective exercises to help open and strengthen your heart even more.

As you read through the exercises, you will notice that the steps are actually quite simple and natural. Being guided by your feeling as you begin to practice, you will experience the beautiful ease of allowing your heart to lead you.

I began presenting Open Heart and Inner Heart workshops years ago, and have been asked why I am writing this book about the heart for the public now. It's because everything is happening at such a fast rate during this spiritual awakening age. In fact, it was not until just several months ago that without any preparation (i.e., Heart workshops), people were able to open and strengthen their hearts easily. Given this great shift and Blessing, this book will be valuable for everyone—including those who have no background whatsoever in heart training or meditation.

May you find everything I share in this book useful. By opening and using your heart more, you will become happier, more peaceful, and healthier. May you also enjoy praying more, be more grateful, and become closer to True Source.

Irmansyah Effendi

Perth, Australia, May 2010

1

OUR HEART

There are countless sayings recognizing the importance of our heart:

"Your vision will become clear only when you look into your heart. Who looks outside, dreams. Who looks inside, awakens."

~ CARL JUNG

"Few are those who see with their own eyes and feel with their own hearts."

~ ALBERT EINSTEIN

"Educating the mind without educating the heart is no education at all."

~ ARISTOTLE

"The only lasting beauty is the beauty of the heart."

~ RUMI

"The worst prison would be a closed heart."

~ POPE JOHN PAUL II

"Wherever you go, go with all your heart."

~ CONFUCIUS

"One learns through the heart, not the eyes or the intellect."

~ MARK TWAIN

"Without a rich heart, wealth is an ugly beggar."

~ RALPH WALDO EMERSON

"It is only with the heart that one can see rightly; what is essential is invisible to the eye."

~ ANTOINE DE SAINT-EXUPERY

"The way is not in the sky. The way is in the heart."

~ BUDDHA

"The best and most beautiful things in the world cannot be seen or even touched. They must be felt with the heart."

~ HELEN KELLER

"In prayer, it is better to have a heart without words than words without a heart."

~ MAHATMA GANDHI

"There is a light that shines beyond all things on Earth, beyond us all, beyond the very highest heavens. This is the light that shines in our heart."

~ CHANDOGYA UPANISHAD 3.13.7

In reading these quotes, we recognize a core essence of truth. There's a knowing and familiarity, despite perhaps never having studied or followed these figures or their stories. That's your heart speaking.

The heart, in its depth, is the center of peace and calmness. When we open and use our heart, we experience genuine lightness and tranquility throughout our whole self.

Sakyamuni Buddha taught: "Calmness is within you; do not look for it outside of you." Yet you don't have to be a Buddha to see how those who chase down worldly success in an effort to be happy and peaceful many times end up anything but. A number of wealthy people find it difficult, often impossible, to smile freely or feel any real calmness or peace in their daily life. If we neglect our heart, we may attain success and material goods, but serenity and happiness will always still be in front of us, just out of reach.

When we open and use our heart properly, by contrast, we find that contentment and pleasure come hand-in-hand with the wealth: helping us to enjoy everything better, and with real perspective. We also share our happiness with those around us more freely, and create an environment that encourages and supports this peace and calmness.

By opening and using our heart in our daily lives, moreover, we can feel and enjoy this peace and calmness—*so clearly*—that our whole heart and our whole self are happy each moment. Your heart, in fact, already knows how. It's only a matter of opening it up and using it.

WHY OUR HEART?

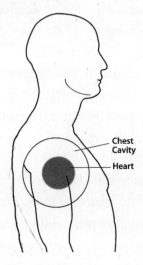

Figure 1. Our heart within the chest cavity

Why is our heart the center of happy and beautiful feelings? Why is our heart, not our brain or other parts of us, the key?

Our heart is the key because our spirit, or our *true self*, is within our heart. The Creator, True Source, is a Spirit, and therefore our true self is also a spirit—a spark of True Source. Our heart is the special facility provided so that there is always a beautiful connection between True Source and the beloved children of True Source.

Our brain is also a wonderful facility given by True Source so that we can learn through experience, as our lessons here on Earth to help us to remember about and choose True Source. But of course it is the special tool, the heart, which has been provided for us to truly improve our connection.

In the same way we must use our eyes to see and our hands to touch—not just intending to or thinking about seeing or touching—our heart must actually be used to strengthen our connection to True Source. Yet because our relationship is obviously not a physical matter but a spiritual one, it's clear that we wouldn't use a physical organ to grow closer to True Source. Again, this is what the heart, the key to our connection, is for. And while the spiritual heart is non-physical, it isn't difficult at all to use; you will see this after opening your heart for some time.

In fact, when our brain chooses True Source, but we also properly use the special facility that has been given to us—our heart—to connect to True Source, True Source's Love can help our spirit directly with everything that is needed. This is part of the beautiful gift of the human body.

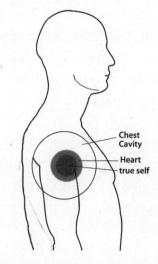

Figure 2. Our true self within our heart

OUR HEART IS THE CENTER OF PEACE, CALMNESS, AND TRUE LOVE

When we open our heart, we recognize and realize the presence of True Source's Blessings. We can feel—really and actually *feel*—so many beautiful things within our heart, including lightness, calmness, peace, happiness, and joy beyond all things we have ever felt from our worldly experiences.

Moments when we are enjoying the feeling from our heart are moments we are actually *using* our heart, letting True Source's Blessing work better on our whole heart and our whole self. Every moment we spend within the Blessing within our heart brings us closer to True Source—to the eternal beauty and joy that our heart already knows, and that our brain has been seeking.

OUR HEART KNOWS THE TRUTH

For ages it has been said we should follow our heart, that our heart knows the truth. Why? This is because our true self, the spark of True Source, within our heart has its own consciousness. This consciousness is much higher than our brain consciousness, and it knows the real truth—what is best for us and for others.

As soon as we use our heart properly, we can realize truths from our own heart, which are better than "truths" from our limited brain. Oftentimes, these aren't truths at all, but what we later find are mistakes based on limited or false information, misjudgments, or poor reasoning.

OTHER SPECIAL THINGS
ABOUT OUR HEART

While the brain is easily influenced by its surroundings, our heart cannot be manipulated by anyone else. The truths from our heart are just that: truths untouched and untouchable by circumstance, persuasion, ego, or any other outside force.

Rather, we and True Source are the only ones who can affect our heart; no other being has the power to make our heart dirty except ourselves. Thus, when we feel hurt, angry, sad, or experience any other negative emotion, we must remind ourselves that it isn't really our colleagues, friends, family, or adverse life events causing these emotions within us. It's actually *us* following the negativity, allowing it to make our heart dirty.

In cleansing and opening our heart, however, it's not enough to rely on our own effort. Just as we're vulnerable to outside forces, we also lack the internal strength to rid ourselves completely of this negative energy. The best way—the most beautiful and joyful way—to cleanse and open our heart, instead, is to ask True Source for blessings. We will practice this later in the book.

2

OPENING & USING OUR HEART

OPENING AND USING OUR HEART WELL IN REALITY

There is a difference between thinking that we have used our heart well, and *actually* using our heart well in practice.

When we are using our heart well in reality, everything becomes more wonderful:

- We can really feel the difference between an ordinary smile and a smile from our heart. When we smile from our heart, we can feel how True Source's Blessing radiates from our heart toward all directions, filling us with a light, calm, peaceful, and beautiful feeling.
- When we smile to our own heart, True Source's Blessing within our heart also radiates so

wonderfully, uplifting our whole heart and feeling to become lighter and more beautiful.

- When we call out to True Source from our heart, we can feel our heart expand, pulling upward. This is our heart praying to True Source.

THE BENEFITS OF OPENING OUR HEART TO TRUE SOURCE

In opening our heart to True Source, we receive so many wonderful benefits. Not only does it make our lives more joyful and fulfilling, but it also improves our spiritual growth. With an open heart:

- Our connection to True Source becomes more beautiful.
- We are able to pray from within our heart.
- We are able to do good deeds with love.
- We are more grateful for everything.
- We surrender more.
- We feel light, calm, and joyful.
- We are far from stress.
- We find it easy to smile from our heart.
- We are mentally, physically, and emotionally healthy.
- We recognize the real truth (True Source's Will).

By opening our heart to True Source, all important matters related to our connection to True Source—which, of course, affects our entire life—will change for the better.

First, our connection will improve. The beauty of praying from the heart will be realized and experienced so clearly, filling our whole heart, our whole self, and our whole feeling.

Our gratitude will also grow and flourish with an open heart. Not only will we become more thankful for True Source's Love and Blessings, but we'll come to enjoy and be more grateful for everything in our lives: from our relationships to our health to our work.

And with an open heart, we are able to smile more easily and more often from our heart. Science, of course, has long shown that a regular smile (not even a smile from our heart) is already good in reducing stress. When we smile from our heart, though, we actually become mentally, physically, and emotionally healthier.

Indeed, recognizing that True Source has blessed us with exactly what will help us grow and learn the most, we are able to open our hearts easily.

3

OUR BRAIN & OUR HEART

How wonderful and exciting it is to know that peace, calmness, happiness and other beautiful feelings are within us at this very moment. To be able to feel and enjoy these blessings, all we need to do is open and begin strengthening our heart.

Toward helping us understand our heart better, there are two important initial steps: First, we need to know the differences between our brain and our heart. Then, we need to recognize the real feeling from our heart.

After learning more about the relationship between the heart and the brain, as well as recognizing how beautiful it feels to be within our heart, we will be able to do many wonderful things for our heart, including:

- Strengthening our heart.
- Lessening our brain's domination.
- Opening our heart through the Open Heart Meditation.

- Realizing the presence of True Source's Blessing in our heart.
- Surrendering our problems and burdens to True Source.
- Relying on True Source's Blessing within our heart when praying and living our daily life.
- Letting our heart take control.

When done wholeheartedly and properly, you will begin to enjoy all of the benefits we have discussed, such as feeling calm, light, and peaceful in your daily life, and realizing how your connection to True Source through your heart is stronger and more beautiful.

I will elaborate on each of these processes throughout the book, presenting not only explanations of the benefits, but easy steps to follow and refer to. These are not new techniques for your heart. In fact, the ways to open and use your heart presented in this book, while detailed and special, are actually quite natural.

USING OUR BRAIN VS. USING OUR HEART AND FEELING

Since the earliest years of our childhood, we have been taught to—and praised for—using and relying on our brain. In fact, the educational systems in most countries are based on strengthening and testing our mental acuity.

So in order to learn more about our heart, to use it properly, we need to start differentiating between what we experience from our brain and what we experience from our heart. Only then will we be able to really get to know our heart:

to begin trusting the truths we feel rather than the ideas we think, imagine, and invent. By following our heart, letting it guide us through the most difficult decisions in our lives and the simplest, we can experience calm, happiness, and security in everything we do.

Brain vs. Heart

The brain is of course the center of our thoughts, while the heart is the center of our feeling (which is actually different from "emotions," as we'll see in the next chapter). Nonetheless, our brain leads our activities and dominates our attention for the vast majority of our waking day, if not all of it.

As we begin to understand the benefits of using our heart more often, and would like to become better aware of the differences between our brain and our heart, let us look at some activities where either our head or our heart is leading the way.

Using Our Brain and Thoughts

Though we're usually not consciously aware, it's obvious that we use our brain whenever we:

- Think
- Talk
- Listen
- Write
- Count
- Move
- Walk
- Drive
- See

- Taste
- Touch
- Smell

Basically, that's just about everything we as human beings do. From the moment we wake up to the moment we go back to sleep, our brain is controlling and regulating our actions, habits, and routines.

We all have responsibilities to fulfill, and we clearly couldn't carry them out without our brains. But in doing our daily activities—whenever and wherever we are—instead of relying entirely on our brain, we need to start allowing our heart the opportunity to share its insights and wisdom.

Using Our Heart and Feeling

Before going further, let us now compare how often our heart and feeling are actually at work:

- How often do you experience the calm and joyful feeling from your heart—not using the five physical senses?
- How often do you realize truths from the heart— knowings that you feel, instead of answers that you conclude or deduce?
- How often do you rely on True Source's Blessing with your heart?

Compared to the amount of time each day we spend using our brain, these total to mere moments for most people. This is true even when praying, which should be an obvious activity for the heart.

Yet praying does not automatically mean we're using our heart and feeling. Very often, prayers are recited from memory using only the brain, which is so limited.

Once you're able to feel the differences, you will realize how important and beautiful it is to pray with sincerity and love from the heart. Then you will want to keep that feeling with you as you go about your everyday activities. Even sitting in traffic can become a joyful experience!

AN EXPERIMENT IN USING OUR BRAIN AND USING OUR HEART

To begin really feeling the differences between when and how our brain and our heart are at work, let's do a little experiment.

For the best results, complete the following exercises (both A and B consecutively) when you have plenty of time, and can relax so that you don't rush through them.

Exercise A: Letting Our Brain Work

Solve the math problems below without using a calculator, and without stopping from one calculation to the next.

- What number is one half of one quarter of one tenth of 400?
- If you count from one to 100, how many sevens will you pass along the way?
- If two typists can type two pages in two minutes, how many typists will it take to type eighteen pages in six minutes?

Realize which part of you is at work, and realize how you feel.

Can you feel pressure or at least some heaviness in your forehead area? This is because the brain within your head is at work.

Exercise B: Letting Our Heart Work

Recall the most beautiful or joyful moment you have ever experienced. Relive that wonderful moment for a while (you don't need to focus on the details of the event; just re-experience what you were feeling at that time).

Realize which part of you is at work and how you feel.

Can you feel a light, happy, joyful feeling in your chest area? This is because your non-physical heart in the center of your chest is at work.

Repeat this experiment until you can clearly feel the differences between using your brain and using your heart.

Once you're able to, it becomes obvious that the more we use our brains and thoughts, the heavier we feel, whereas the more we use our heart, the lighter, calmer, and happier we feel.

Yes, but can you really compare doing math problems to the happiest moment of your life? Not directly, of course; but the feelings that the two activities produce are consistent across experiences. This means that the more you are in your heart while completing your daily activities, the more peaceful and joyful you will feel. Soon, you won't have to recall anything to experience these wonderful feelings in your heart.

THE REAL FEELING

Just as it is important to distinguish between the work of our brain and the work of our heart, it's essential we recognize the differences between the real feeling from our heart, and emotions and sensations that come from elsewhere.

The emotions we experience throughout the day—in addition to all of the other perceptions and reactions our body signals to us—are not feelings from our heart. Surprisingly, even those emotions we normally attribute to our heart don't arise from there at all. In fact, you've probably never considered "feelings" in the way we'll look at them here.

FEELINGS AND SENSATIONS THAT ARE NOT FROM THE HEART

If you were asked to describe a cat's tongue or a back massage, you'd probably say, "it *feels* rough" or "it *feels* good." You might even say of loud music, "it *feels* harsh."

We feel the cat's tongue as coarse when it makes contact with our skin; we feel a release as the pressures from the massage are applied to our muscles. We use the word "feel" simply to describe what we experience from our five physical senses. Since these are what we most often perceive, this is how we tend to frame, catalog, and understand our life encounters.

We commonly sense a number of other internal cues from the body that don't originate in our heart. Most familiar, perhaps, is the sensation of feeling tired: Surely we know when we are, and there are plenty of associated physical expressions, including weak muscles, heavy eyelids, and lapses in concentration. Your heart is not tired, though; only your body is.

In heart exercises, when we use the term "feel," please don't confuse it with the messages coming from our five physical senses or internally from the body. Although you'll naturally want to look for these tangible and familiar physical experiences, do your best to resist the inclination. The real feeling from the heart, while clear and powerful, does not manifest in ways you're used to.

You might take this opportunity now, before beginning our heart practices, to start releasing your brain from focusing on the signals it normally picks up on. Even while remaining aware, by not actively watching what's happening throughout your body, you give your brain a chance to relax. Being relaxed will be key to being present and fully enjoying the heart exercises.

"Feeling" That Comes from Our Brain

Besides the responses our body sends us from the environment, our mind also plays an integral part in guiding our awareness. Feeling bored from having to wait in line or do a repetitive task at work, for example, is a familiar experience to us—for some, all too familiar. As our interest and curiosity wane, thoughts drift, and we grow antsy and impatient. This is our head in motion, constantly creating and feeding us with signals and perceptions.

Our heart, by contrast, is never bored, impatient, edgy, or anything of the like. These are just mental constructions that arise from an under- or overactive brain. So please don't confuse feelings of this sort, either, with the feeling from your heart, which radiates only feel-good sensations such as happiness, calmness, and peace.

In this vein, it's important here to point out another common experience that comes from the brain: the feeling of dislike toward someone. It's undeniable that we feel it, whether or not we intend to, or whether we even approve of the emotion. And since we perceive feelings of "like" as coming from the heart, we naturally assume the opposite feelings would arise from the same place. But in doing so, we make a fundamental error that can cause us to not only misunderstand our heart, but prevent us from allowing it to open fully and completely.

"Feeling" That Comes from Emotions

This person we feel dislike toward has likely caused us certain kinds of emotional difficulties or pain, from as little as irritation and dissatisfaction up to genuine anger or resentment.

When we are "feeling" sad or angry, however, the sadness and the anger are actually *emotions* that come from our solar plexus; *not* our heart. The next time you experience strong or excessive negative emotions, pay attention to where you feel the negativity originating from. You can clearly feel the pressure, or even pain, in your solar plexus area—just below your chest cavity, sometimes radiating down to the stomach.

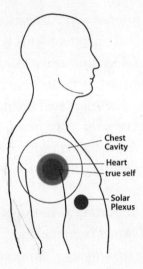

Figure 3. Solar plexus: the center of emotions

These kinds of negative emotions are important examples of what is *not* the real feeling from our heart. While it's common to talk about a "broken heart" or an "angry heart," such concepts are opposite and incompatible with the feeling from your heart. But because people feel they experience romantic love from the heart (which is not true of roller-coaster infatuation and lust), they likewise believe loss and hurt is experienced in their heart, as well.

While the other feelings and sensations we've discussed up to now are relatively shallow in that they deal with the physical senses or normal activities of the brain, emotions are quite deep. What's so consequential about emotions is that every time we have a bad one, we are actually creating negativities and placing them in our heart. There they accumulate, causing our heart to become dirty and closed.

How dirty and closed? Well, think about the last time you felt annoyed, angry, sad, jealous, envious, hurt, arrogant, guilty, cunning, greedy, and so on. Also consider the stresses and irritations of our daily lives, and all the negative emotions we experience on a regular, recurring basis (e.g., commuting, conflicts at work, disagreements at home, etc.). Even when you don't express any of these emotions explicitly, the instant you feel them, the negativities have already been created and are amassing in your heart.

Of course, if we choose not to follow the negative emotion or allow it to dwell in us, the negativities placed in our heart are not as great as when we indulge and linger. But regardless, any upsetting, unhappy, or unpleasant emotion will make our heart dirty in some way.

Just imagine all the negative emotions you've experienced not only recently in your everyday life, but from the beginning of our existence as we know it. Without deeply and regularly cleansing our heart, can you even conceptualize how much "junk" has accumulated over all this time? Again, because it's all too common for people to credit negative emotions as feelings from the heart, I would like to pause here to further clarify the differences between emotions and the real feeling from our heart.

"EMOTIONS" VS. "FEELING"

Emotions

I use the term "emotions" to describe those hurtful and distressing reactions we experience, which create negativities that collect in our heart—making our heart dirty and, if not properly cleansed, closing our heart.

Examples of emotions include:

- Anger
- Hatred
- Resentment
- Irritation
- Sadness
- Dissatisfaction
- Jealousy / envy
- Arrogance
- Greediness / cunningness
- Any other negative or unpleasant sentiment

To understand how easily emotions can affect us, consider our earlier example of growing bored from waiting too long in line. As the boredom mounts, we begin to feel tense, and this tension keeps on building with time as we wait longer. During the process, we usually also start to feel tired, uneasy, and a little anxious. Still, at this point we have not yet affected our heart. But as we continue to follow the boredom downward, the second we let it turn into irritation, it becomes an emotion, creating negativities in our heart.

Varieties of this scenario are so common, in so many instances of our lives. It's so ordinary, in fact, that we're scarcely aware it has even happened and soon forget we were ever irritated.

Feeling

I use the term "feeling," by contrast, only to refer to the real feelings from our heart—which are the good and wonderful sensations that surface in our heart, and radiate out to the rest of our being.

Examples of feelings are:

- **Love**
- Peace
- Calmness
- Beauty
- Happiness
- Joy
- Any other feel-good and uplifting sentiment

When we experience any of these feelings, our heart expands, and we become light and joyful. If you are sensitive, you can actually perceive your heart growing bigger and stronger, as your chest fills with a relaxed, happy, peaceful feeling. This is a wonderful indication we are using and enjoying the real feeling from our heart properly.

To expand on this point, we specially call out "love" from the list above for a couple of important reasons. First, please don't mistake explosive emotions, such as the up-and-down swings of infatuation and lust, for real love from your heart. If you have experienced these emotions before, you know that they are not calm, gentle, or patient—characteristics of real love.

Relatedly, some participants in my past workshops have voiced concerns about opening their hearts: worried they'll become vulnerable and get hurt more easily in life as a result of opening their hearts to give and share their love better.

While that is a perfectly normal apprehension, I assure you our heart is the center of only happy and beautiful feelings, so there are absolutely no adverse effects in opening and using your heart more. In fact, as your heart grows bigger and stronger—as you learn to be within your heart more deeply and more often—you will actually become *less* susceptible to the negative emotional consequences of life situations.

So please don't worry about opening and using your heart. This beautiful, natural process will begin to cleanse and purify your heart of all the negativities that have accumulated for so long. You will be filled with calmness, joy, and many other wonderful feelings in your daily life, and praying will also become deeper and more beautiful.

In the end, this is really about strengthening your connection to True Source—which can only make everything in your life better, happier, and more fulfilling.

5

IMPORTANT KEYS IN USING YOUR HEART

Up to this point, we have been laying the conceptual foundation to help you better understand your heart. Now, to better prepare you for the actual heart practices, we'll go deeper into the steps, ways, and principles for activating and using your heart.

THE TWO BASIC PRINCIPLES IN OPENING AND USING YOUR HEART

Our heart is a beautiful Gift of Love from True Source, and only awaits us to open, use, and enjoy it. We once knew how, so well and so naturally: when we were little children and lived with near-continuous joy, curiosity, freedom, and peace.

But then we "grew up"—psychologically more importantly than physically—and were directed to, and rewarded for, using our brain to make decisions and solve problems. The heart, which once guided us easily, was made to be quiet by parents, teachers, and other authority figures. Reason, logic, and rule-based systems began to shape our growth and development.

This shift led to a sharp imbalance in the rates of development between our brain and our heart, which is at the core of the problem: Over time, much like a physical response from using one part the body more than another, our minds have grown stronger as our hearts have grown weaker.

With our brain blocking our heart—constantly generating harmful emotions that create negativities in our heart, without allowing it to open up to be cleansed—our heart becomes heavier, dirtier, and more closed by the accumulated negativities.

This has been the case for a very long time. Yet, knowing what we now know about the heart as the center of peace, calmness, and joy, we can begin the process and journey of allowing it to be cleansed, opened, and used to guide and support us.

The heart exercises in this book are a wonderful and important first step in this process. Let us start with two important keys to the practice:

1. Do not let your brain block your heart.
2. Allow your heart be free naturally on its own.

1. Do not let your brain block your heart.

We are bombarded by our thoughts. With overscheduled and socially complicated lives, we are constantly remembering and reminding ourselves of our responsibilities, relationships, issues, and burdens. Ongoing personal and professional demands often make it feel impossible to really be present in the current moment, much less enjoy it.

The good news is, we have our heart to connect to True Source, the Source of peace, calmness, and joy. So just relax and let go of all of the tensions in your body. Go ahead and take a few moments to do that now…

Completely relaxed? Clear mind? Hmm, probably not yet. As human beings, we're not only extremely practiced at using our brain, but also have remarkably little ability to control our thoughts. In fact, the more we try to push a thought out of our head, the more invasively present the thought becomes—thanks to the automatic process of our mind repeatedly checking whether or not the thought is still there.

Still, relaxing the body can help you a lot in letting go of the chatter in the brain. Like most any other skill, it will become more natural and enjoyable with time and practice and as you feel the results work.

2. Allow your heart be free naturally on its own.

When you are relaxed and your brain isn't blocking, your heart will be free naturally on its own. So in order to get things going, we need to stimulate our heart by beginning a good heart habit… A smiling habit!

Smile freely, easily, and happily. All the time.

When you regularly allow yourself to smile freely and happily, it becomes a normal way of being, and your heart will become free all on its own.

As you begin to cultivate this wonderful practice, you may notice you actually find it difficult to smile, odd as that may sound. But we can see that children smile and laugh much more easily and often than the average adult, meaning even something as easy and pleasurable as turning up your cheeks may take some consideration and practice.

To help grow your awareness, pay attention to others you meet throughout the course of the day. You'll notice some people tend to smile more freely, laugh more easily, and keep a joyful disposition and outlook. Smile more the way they do, and you will keep on stimulating your heart. Remembering you have nothing to lose by choosing to be lighter, in no time your heart will become freer.

The two basic principles of opening and using your heart, then, are not letting your brain block your heart, and allowing your heart be free naturally on its own. We accomplish these simply by relaxing better and smiling more—both of which are natural and enjoyable behaviors most of us would like to do more of anyway. Opening our heart is actually a very familiar and wonderful process!

THE FOUR KEY STEPS IN DOING HEART EXERCISES

Now that we understand why we want our brain to be "off" and our heart to be open and free, there are four key steps to follow while doing the heart exercises:

1. Relax
2. Close your eyes
3. Touch your heart
4. Smile to your heart

The first two steps may seem obvious, and the second two a little curious; but as you'll read, there are important reasons for each. Once more, these are actually very natural practices for your heart, which you will be able to feel clearly as you follow the process.

1. Relax

As discussed, we want our brain to be relaxed such that it doesn't block our heart. So besides not following your thoughts (i.e., not giving the thoughts that do surface any focus or attention), there is no need to put in any effort whatsoever when doing the heart exercises. The harder we try, the less we're able to receive—because trying activates the brain. When it comes to the heart, less is truly more.

Of course, relaxing means mind *and* body. Now, you want your spine to be straight when you do the heart exercises, so the energy can flow smoothly; but your muscles should never be tense. Usually you can find a chair that comfortably supports the way you sit while still allowing your spine to be straight as you remain relaxed. You can even try sitting against a wall with pillows.

But don't limit how relaxed you can be. We're often unaware certain muscles remain tightened, or that we're still holding someplace when we think we're perfectly relaxed. Just feel your shoulders right now, and allow them drop; were you even aware of the tension there? So whenever you feel nicely relaxed, simply relax even more and notice where you feel additional releases. Repeat again, and realize you continue to let go and become more relaxed.

2. Close Your Eyes

We know from experience that closing our eyes helps our brain to be more relaxed. Although we'll sometimes shut our eyes when deep in concentration, more generally we close them (automatically) to rest or sleep. Regardless, in both cases we're blocking outside visual stimuli from activating our mind.

By closing your eyes during heart exercises, your brain isn't busy processing any visual information, which allows it to become more relaxed.

3. Touch Your Heart

Because we so seldom use our heart in our daily life, physically touching our heart helps to awaken and activate it, as well as keep us focused on the feelings from the heart during our exercises.

To find your heart, extend your arm out, level with your shoulder, and trace a line back to the center of your chest, at the same height as your underarm. Touch your heart at that center of your chest with one or more fingers or your palm, using either the right or left hand. From there, simply enjoy feeling your heart: using the touch to help keep from paying attention to any thoughts or distractions that may arise.

4. Smile to Your Heart

That's right, smile to your heart! Don't think about how or what it might look like to others; just smile sweetly and freely to your heart. Feel how easy and nice it is—feel how your heart grows stronger and more dominant as you smile even sweeter and freer.

This is because smiling is so very natural to our heart. By smiling, we're helping our heart to be free and to return to its joyful state of being.

While smiling to your heart, don't concern yourself with visualizing how, and do not bend your neck to look at your heart, which will disrupt your relaxed body position. As we'll discuss next, visualizing activates the brain. Even if you feel like it's helping, it actually blocks your heart.

COMMON MISTAKES IN DOING HEART EXERCISES

Knowing what *not* to do, certainly, is just as important as knowing what we should do. Now that we've covered the four key steps in practicing heart exercises, let's also look at the two most common mistakes people tend to make—which, as you might guess, deal with our brain taking control.

While our brain manages our body, our connection to True Source is governed by our heart, which has its own consciousness and will work naturally by itself the moment we relax and smile to it.

Mistake 1. Your Brain Trying to Open the Door to Your Heart

As if by reflex, many who begin the process of opening their heart try to do so by visualizing their heart actually opening.

The act of visualizing is done by the brain, which gives it yet another chance to block the heart. Even though this practice might help someone become calmer—much like any other meditation that focuses on breathing, chanting, or the like—using your mind to picture any kind of metaphor for opening your heart will only serve to slow or stop the process.

Simply relax, smile, and enjoy: let your heart open naturally on its own.

Mistake 2. Your Brain Trying to Strengthen Your Heart / Feeling

In Chapter 3, you did an experiment to feel the differences between when your brain was at work and when your heart was at work. To continue with the experiment here, please go back and complete the "Letting Our Heart Work" portion of the exercise once more, and then return to this page…

Now, as you're experiencing the warm, joyful feeling in your chest, try to strengthen that nice, pleasant feeling. What do you feel? If you're sensitive, you'll actually experience some pressure on your heart.

The moment your brain tries to strengthen your heart / feeling, it restricts your heart from being free on its own. So instead of having the pleasant, happy feeling more pronounced, you actually feel uncomfortable and distracting pressures.

Heart practices, while natural, are quite different from how you're accustomed to approaching things. Just give it some time, follow the steps in the heart exercises as closely as possible—using the basic principles, key points, and suggestions—and your heart and feeling will be stronger in no time.

6

STRENGTHENING YOUR HEART

It's now time to move from theory into practice, beginning with the first of our heart exercises, Strengthening-of-the-Heart. This basic, yet fundamental, heart exercise will begin the wonderful process of awakening your heart.

In addition to step-by-step instructions, we will also go over tips, hints, and common mistakes, along with other important matters related to this exercise. But, as always, the best and most valuable thing you can do—not only during this heart exercise, but all the time—is to relax…smile…and enjoy!

STRENGTHENING-OF-THE-HEART EXERCISE

The Strengthening-of-the-Heart exercise, while simple, is very deep and important. It will help you to:

1. Focus more on your heart.
2. Lessen your brain's domination.

3. Strengthen your heart and feeling.

To relax your brain, you will be asked to close your eyes; so of course you need to read and remember the steps of this exercise first. As your mind will still be active in recalling the points, it is recommended that you record your voice while reading the steps, or listen to the guided practices available on smiletoyourheart.org.

When doing this or any of the heart exercises, please find a quiet spot where you won't be interrupted or distracted. If you're not practicing as part of a group, being in a private room or space is ideal, so you don't become self-conscious or remain aware of your surroundings.

In choosing a seating position, feel free to sit either on a chair or cross-legged on the floor, whichever is more comfortable for you. Either way, avoid sitting on a cushion that's too soft or otherwise doesn't allow you to remain still. To ensure your spine is straight, but without tensing yourself, make sure your chair or support has a hard, straight back. When you sit with your buttocks as close to the back support as possible, you can comfortably align your spine just by leaning backward.

Now, when you're ready, we'll begin:

1. Close your eyes to reduce the activities of your brain.
2. Completely relax your body and mind.
3. Breathe in deeply through your nose, and exhale through your mouth several times to help you relax even more.
4. Touch your heart with one or more fingers.
5. Smile freely to your heart without thinking how.
6. With your eyes still closed and staying relaxed, smile to your heart for about one minute. When you find yourself thinking, don't follow your thoughts; just relax and allow them to pass easily through your head.

7. Gradually, you should start experiencing an expansion in your chest area, along with feelings of calmness, peacefulness, lightness, or joy.

8. When you feel any of these nice feelings, it's a wonderful indication that your heart is starting to work. Just follow the pleasant feeling to let your heart and feeling become even stronger.

9. If you're not feeling anything yet, don't put in any effort whatsoever. Simply stay relaxed and keep on smiling. The moment your brain stops trying and looking for sensations, you will be able to feel one or more of the nice feelings.

10. Relax even better and smile more freely.

11. Once you start experiencing the calmness, lightness, or joy, follow your feeling while continuing to relax and smile (two minutes or more).

As you can see, this is an easy and straightforward—yet very deep and important—exercise that can help strengthen your heart and the feeling from your heart.

The Benefits of Being Guided

As a beginner, if you do the heart exercises on your own, you may very well start off doing them properly. But then your brain may kick in, looking for feelings or sensations before your heart gets a chance to react.

When you are guided by someone with experience in heart practices or those who have taken the Open Heart workshops, on the other hand, they will help you to remain relaxed and undistracted, so that your heart has a chance to become stronger—where you can then feel the nice feelings naturally. Those well-practiced in heart exercises can also tell you if you're not relaxed or smiling enough, if you're observing, or if you're making any other mistakes. (And of course they will also tell you when you're doing it right)!

Certainly, it's not compulsory to seek out help; you can do all of the exercises on your own without being guided by those who have done the Open Heart workshops. What you should remember, though, is that it takes time to strengthen your heart and feeling—even when you're doing the exercises well by yourself. Just keep on practicing, and give your heart and feeling some time to grow stronger.

If You Do Not Feel Anything

This whole "feeling" business has become a problem for some. They want to feel the nice feeling so much that they end up putting in effort and becoming tense—which, of course, just activates the brain and blocks the heart. Trying harder has precisely the opposite effect of what's intended.

So please let go of any effort in wanting to feel something; it will come easily and naturally when you're relaxed enough. In the meantime, know that even when you're not fully experiencing the sensations, your heart still receives wonderful benefits. Just do the heart exercises as best you can: letting yourself be as relaxed as possible, smiling freely, and simply enjoying the moment.

You should also know that those who try so much and keep saying they don't feel anything actually *have* felt the feeling from their heart. They're just not familiar enough with it to be able to recognize what they're experiencing—looking for something closer to what they know from their five physical senses.

Rather, the feeling from our heart is calm and gentle. It doesn't necessarily seem "real" at first. In fact, many people question whether what they're feeling is actually coming from their heart at all. This is quite normal, but another case of trying too hard. In general, if you feel something light, calm, peaceful, expansive, and happy, then you're experiencing the feeling from your heart.

Do this Strengthening-of-the-Heart exercise regularly and frequently, not only to strengthen your heart but to also help you recognize the gentle feeling from your heart. Repeating this practice daily (ideally, several times a day) will be especially good for those of you who have difficulty feeling at the beginning. Just remember the keys—relax, smile freely, and simply enjoy—and you'll get there soon enough.

To that point, each and every exercise presented in this book will help you strengthen your heart and feeling. But this Strengthening-of-the-Heart practice is really the core technique, and needs to be done well in order to move on properly to the next exercises.

CORRECTING MISTAKES

Beginners tend to make four common mistakes that slow their progress and limit the results from the heart exercises:

1. Bending the neck or looking down
2. Looking for sensations or wanting results
3. Following thoughts
4. Being distracted and influenced by outside noises

So let's have a closer look at each of these, and see where and how we can make some easy corrections.

1. Bending the Neck or Looking Down

When you bend your neck or look down, you lose your relaxed, comfortable body position. This makes it easy for your brain to block your heart. It also causes your neck and upper back to become tired and sore.

So please be aware of your head and neck position when first starting your heart practices, and be sure to straighten your upper-body posture so that everything is comfortably aligned.

This also applies to looking up too much, which isn't necessary. Just pull up your chin a little bit and let your head be in a normal position. Someone who's experienced with heart practices can also help you find the right posture.

2. Looking for Sensations or Wanting Results

As we have discussed at length, looking for sensations means the mind is working. The more you *want* to feel, the less you will actually end up feeling. It's a system that runs counter to our typical effort–results paradigm, which works only for our brain—not our heart.

As soon as you relax and smile freely, and your heart is free from the brain's blocking, you will feel the pleasant feelings from your heart again.

3. Following Thoughts

Having thoughts, of course, is a normal and ongoing part of being human. We're so used to thinking—it's so automatic—that even when we don't need or want our thoughts, there they are.

So it's inevitable that thoughts will find their way into your head while practicing the heart exercises. When they do, simply don't follow the thoughts. Just let them pass and keep your attention on the wonderful feelings from your heart.

This can be difficult for some, but please don't worry. As long as you do not follow the thoughts, stay relaxed, and continue to smile sweetly and freely to your heart, you are doing great.

4. Letting Outside Noise Influence and Distract You

It's also common for those new to heart exercises to still be influenced and distracted by surrounding noise and activity. Physiologically, of course, we're "wired" to pay attention to what's happening in our environment.

But outside attention and awareness are the domain of the brain. Since your heart is blocked when your mind is watching what's happening around you (even if not with your eyes), it's important that you allow your surroundings to be just that: Let whatever noise or movement in your environment exist only in your environment, not in your brain.

When you do find yourself distracted, just smile even more freely to your heart, and allow the feeling from your heart to become dominant again. In time, as your heart strengthens, the noise and movement from your surroundings won't influence you anymore.

IMPORTANT MATTERS RELATED TO HEART EXERCISES

Before we move on to the next exercise, there are some key points to keep in mind as you begin your heart practices:

- Exercising your heart is not the same as dancing or singing, where only those who are talented can do well. Everyone has a heart, and everyone can use it wonderfully.

- For those of you who are "thinkers" and tend to use your mind excessively, it may take you a longer time to relax into the feeling from your heart. But don't succumb to the difficulty or frustration; using your heart will be quite natural after you "shift," and this isn't a productive or proper attitude to approach with. Instead, just keep on practicing the heart exercises without putting in any effort or giving attention to your brain when it tries to interfere.

- Some of you will be able to feel something in your first attempts, while others will need more practice to experience the feeling from the heart. So if you don't feel anything even after several practices of the exercises, please don't worry; this only means you're not as relaxed as you can be. Also keep in mind that even when you're not feeling anything or don't feel as you expect to, you still receive the benefits. Just keep on practicing and you will make progress.

- When you have difficulty feeling your heart:
  ◊ Don't open your eyes.
  ◊ Don't look for the feeling.
  ◊ Don't stop the exercise, or allow yourself to become frustrated or disappointed.
  ◊ Just stay relaxed and keep on doing the exercise, intending only to enjoy.
  ◊ The sooner you relax properly, the sooner you will feel the feeling from your heart.

- The "feeling" we are talking about here is the calm, gentle feeling from our heart—which is similar to the light feeling you experience when you are happy and joyful. So please don't expect any kind of intense reaction or any kind of physical manifestation, such as the sensation of heat or cold.

- The heart exercises presented in this book are similar, but each one offers something unique and special. As our heart is very deep, the different practices activate and strengthen specific parts of our heart, helping it to open in the best, most complete way possible. So continue doing each individual exercise the best you can—even if you feel that you are able to do the previous one quite well already. Every time you use your heart the best, it opens better and better, without limit.

- All exercises given in this book use natural methods that rely on True Source's Blessing to help stimulate your heart. The main key to every practice is actually surrendering to True Source, from the heart.

7

IMPROVING THE QUALITY OF THE HEART EXERCISES

In Chapter 5, we looked at the two basic principles of opening and using your heart, as well as the four key steps in doing the heart exercises.

Now that we've begun our practices, we are going to repeat the Strengthening-of-the-Heart exercise with variations to better understand the importance of the four key steps, as well as to improve on them by experiencing the differences firsthand.

For the best results, do the exercises in this chapter only after you are able to feel the light, calm, peaceful, happy, joyful, or expansive feeling in your heart. And if you're not there yet, don't worry: Just keep doing it while staying relaxed, smiling, and enjoying.

The four key steps we're focusing on for improvement here are: (1) Relaxing, (2) Closing your eyes, (3) Touching your heart, and (4) Smiling to your heart.

Once you begin to do each key step better, the overall quality of your heart exercises will improve wonderfully, and your heart and feeling will grow even stronger.

STRENGTHENING YOUR HEART: RELAXING VS. NOT RELAXING

Before beginning this practice, please make sure you are sitting properly, as always. Again, you can sit on a chair, a couch, cross-legged on the floor, or whatever suits you best. Just see to it that your spine is always straight, but without tensing yourself. This is to ensure that the energy flow throughout your body is smooth and uninterrupted.

Find a nice and quiet spot where you won't be distracted or disturbed. If you're practicing on your own, a private room or space is always preferred, so you can really let go without being self-aware or concerned with your surroundings.

Once you're seated correctly and comfortably, you can start the Strengthening-of-the-Heart exercise with the relaxing / not relaxing variation:

1. Close your eyes to reduce the activities of your brain.
2. Completely relax your body and mind.
3. Breathe in deeply through your nose, and exhale through your mouth several times to help you relax even more.
4. Touch your heart with one or more fingers.
5. Smile freely to your heart without thinking how.
6. Still relaxed, with your eyes still closed, smile to your heart (for about one minute). When you find yourself

thinking, don't follow your thoughts. Just relax and let them pass easily through your head.

7. Gradually, you should start experiencing an expansion in your chest area, along with feelings of calmness, peacefulness, lightness, or joy.

8. When you feel any of these nice feelings, it's a wonderful indication that your heart is starting to work. Just follow this nice, pleasant feeling to let your heart and feeling become even stronger.

9. If you're not feeling anything yet, don't put in any effort whatsoever. Simply stay relaxed and keep on smiling. The moment your brain stops trying and looking for sensations, you will be able to feel one or more of the nice feelings.

10. Relax even better and smile more freely.

11. Once you start experiencing the calm, lightness, or joy, follow your feeling while continuing to relax and smile (one minute or longer).

The next steps must be done with your eyes closed, while still touching your heart and smiling freely to your heart.

12. Now tense your body.

13. If you're sensitive, you will feel how your heart and chest are pressured—or at the very least, that the expanding, light, calm, peaceful, joyful feeling diminishes considerably.

14. Now relax your whole body.

15. If you continue to follow your feeling, you will experience relief the instant you relax your body. Feel how your heart is free from pressure and heaviness as soon as your body is no longer stressed.

16. Tense your body again.

17. Feel the pressure on your heart, and the lessening of the expanding, calm, happy feeling.

18. Now relax your whole body once more.

19. Feel how your heart and feeling are now free from the pressure or heaviness.

20. By tensing and relaxing your body, and experiencing the differences in your feeling, you should be able to better feel the remaining tension in your body. Once you do, completely relax those parts.

21. As soon as your feeling is free from the pressure / heaviness, follow the changes or progress in your heart and feeling. In doing so, your heart and feeling will be even freer from the limitations that your brain has imposed all this time.

22. When this exercise is done properly, you will be able to feel how your heart and feeling have become stronger, deeper, and more enjoyable.

Do this Strengthening-of-the-Heart exercise with the key step of relaxing / not relaxing once or twice a day, until you are able to:

- Relax your whole body until you feel completely calm, peaceful, and free from any tensions; and
- Follow the changes that your heart and feeling experience as they become freer from the limitations of your brain.

STRENGTHENING YOUR HEART: CLOSING YOUR EYES VS. NOT CLOSING YOUR EYES

Closing our eyes should be a straightforward process, obviously. Yet, when you watch people doing the heart exercises, you notice how some of them are able to close their eyes easily while staying relaxed (as you might expect), while others struggle and actually put pressure and focus on their own eyes.

Not only does this clearly prevent you from relaxing, but it also activates the brain, which further blocks your heart and feeling. To understand the process better, we will do the Strengthening-of-the-Heart exercise with the eyes-closed/eyes-open variation, which will help you learn to close your eyes while staying even more relaxed.

Now, when you're ready:

1. Close your eyes to reduce the activities of your brain.
2. Completely relax your body and mind.
3. Breathe in deeply through your nose, and exhale through your mouth several times to help you relax even more.
4. Touch your heart with one or more fingers.
5. Smile freely to your heart without thinking how.
6. With your eyes still closed and staying relaxed, smile to your heart (for about one minute). When you find yourself thinking, don't follow your thoughts. Just relax and allow them to pass easily through your head.
7. Gradually, you should start experiencing an expansion in your chest area, along with feelings of calmness, peacefulness, lightness, or joy.
8. Follow that nice, pleasant feeling to let your heart and feeling become stronger (one minute or longer).

The next steps must be done while staying relaxed, touching your heart, and smiling freely to your heart.

9. Now open your eyes.
10. You should feel that your attention has moved upward from your heart in your chest area, toward your eyes

and your brain. Your heart and feeling are not as strong as before you opened your eyes.

11. Close your eyes again.

12. You will feel that your attention gradually returns to your heart, and that the nice feeling grows stronger.

13. Now close your eyes intently. You will feel pressure not only on both of your eyes, but also on your forehead area—because your brain is also working harder. Instances like these are moments when your brain is limiting your heart and feeling.

14. Knowing this, now close your eyes and relax them completely. Feel that the pressures on your forehead lessen and slowly disappear quite naturally. The feeling from your heart is becoming stronger and stronger.

From now on, please make sure that when you have your eyes closed, you do it in a perfectly relaxed manner like this, without any pressure whatsoever.

STRENGTHENING YOUR HEART: TOUCHING YOUR HEART VS. NOT TOUCHING YOUR HEART

Now we will do the Strengthening-of-the-Heart exercise with the touching / not touching your heart variation, to experience how this affects the practice.

1. Close your eyes to reduce the activities of your brain.

2. Completely relax your body and mind.

3. Breathe in deeply through your nose, and exhale through your mouth several times to help you relax even more.

4. Touch your heart with one or more fingers.

5. Smile freely to your heart without thinking how.

6. With your eyes still closed and staying relaxed, smile to your heart (for about one minute). When you find yourself thinking, don't follow your thoughts: Just relax, and allow them to pass easily through your head.

7. Gradually, you should start experiencing an expansion in your chest area, along with feelings of calm, peace, lightness, or joy.

8. When you feel any of these pleasant feelings, it's a wonderful indication that your heart is starting to work. Just follow the feeling to let it—and your heart—become even stronger.

9. If you're not feeling anything yet, don't put in any effort whatsoever. Simply stay relaxed and keep on smiling. The moment your brain stops trying and looking for sensations, you will be able to feel one or more of the nice feelings.

10. Relax even better and smile more freely.

The next steps must be done while staying relaxed, with your eyes closed and smiling freely to your heart.

11. Now remove your fingers from the center of your chest.

12. Feel how your feeling is diminishing, or is not as clear as it was before removing your fingers.

13. Touch your heart again.

14. Feel how your attention is redirected to your heart, and that your heart and feeling are becoming noticeably stronger.

15. Stop touching your heart again.

16. Realize your feeling is fading once more.

17. Return your fingers to your heart.

18. As soon as your fingers touch your heart, feel clearly how your heart and feeling become deeper and more expansive.

19. Follow the changes from the moment your heart and feeling were not as strong, to the moment they become stronger. By following the changes, you are letting your heart and feeling become stronger in the best way.

Physically touching your heart helps to activate it and keep your attention on all the wonderful feelings.

STRENGTHENING YOUR HEART: SMILING VS. NOT SMILING

In our final variation, we will experience how smiling to your heart and not smiling to your heart impact the Strengthening-of-the-Heart exercise. Again, you might suspect that because smiling is generally natural and spontaneous, it would easily flow as part of the process. Yet at the beginning, it can be normal to feel some resistance, or find that it takes a little practice and awareness to really let your smile be natural and free. (And, no, "smiling on the inside" isn't enough)!

1. Close your eyes to reduce the activities of your brain.
2. Completely relax your body and mind.
3. Breathe in deeply through your nose and exhale through your mouth several times to help you relax even more.
4. Touch your heart with one or more fingers.
5. Smile freely to your heart without thinking how.
6. With your eyes still closed and staying relaxed, smile to your heart (for about one minute). When you find yourself thinking, don't follow your thoughts. Just relax and allow them to pass easily through your head.

7. Gradually, you should start experiencing an expansion in your chest area along with feelings of calmness, peacefulness, lightness, or joy.

8. When you feel any of these nice feelings, it means your heart is starting to work. Just follow the feeling to let your heart and feeling become even stronger.

9. If you're not feeling anything yet, don't put in any effort whatsoever. Simply stay relaxed and keep on smiling. The moment your brain stops trying and looking for sensations, you will be able to feel one or more of the nice feelings.

10. Relax even better and smile more freely.

The next steps must be done while staying relaxed, with your eyes closed and touching your heart.

11. Now stop smiling to your heart.

12. Realize that the feeling you're experiencing in your heart is diminishing, or is even disappearing completely.

13. Smile to your heart once more.

14. Feel how your heart and feeling become stronger, and you are able to feel the expanding, light, happy feeling you felt before.

15. Stop smiling to your heart.

16. Notice how the feeling in your heart lessens or disappears again. Realize that your chest is not as full and light as it was.

17. Smile to your heart again.

18. Feel that your heart and feeling are becoming stronger once again. Notice how the wonderful feelings grow, expand, and radiate.

19. Now smile even more freely to your heart, following your smile and feeling. (Remember, this is the calm,

gentle feeling from your heart; don't look for any explosive emotions).

20. Feel how by smiling more freely, your heart and feeling are becoming even stronger and more enjoyable.

21. Follow the changes from the moment your heart and feeling were not as strong, to the moment they become stronger. Following the changes as you switch back and forth between smiling and not smiling is the best way to let your heart and feeling become stronger.

To smile freely the most natural way, just follow your feeling while continuing to stay relaxed. Don't try too hard to widen or force your smile. Effort will only activate your brain, and you'll begin to feel the tension on your face after smiling too broadly for a while.

Again, smiling properly simply means you are letting the pleasant feeling from your heart grow stronger while just effortlessly enjoying the moment. In fact, the longer you do it, the more refreshed you will feel, without any tension on your face or anywhere else in your body.

STRENGTHENING YOUR HEART: REPEATING PROPERLY

You have just experienced firsthand the importance of each of the four key steps of heart exercises: relaxing completely, closing your eyes, touching your heart, and smiling freely to your heart. When done properly, these will help you open and strengthen your heart and feeling.

Coupled with avoiding the common mistakes we discussed (i.e., bending the neck, looking for results, following thoughts, being distracted by outside noises), you will be able to do the

Strengthening-of-the-Heart exercise more easily, correctly, and enjoyably.

While practicing through these exercise variations, keep in mind that their purpose is to better the quality of your Strengthening-of-the-Heart exercise. Each one, much like resistance training for muscles, works on a different part of your technique. Taken together, this "calisthenics program" for your heart will result in a wonderful overall improvement. Though you may not want to let the beautiful feeling from your heart diminish by, say, tensing your body or not smiling, the lasting outcome far outweighs the temporary loss.

Also, please remember that the Strengthening-of-the-Heart exercise, while simple, is the fundamental foundation for the rest of the heart exercises. Every time you repeat this practice properly, you will strengthen your heart and your feeling.

8

OPEN HEART
MEDITATION

After completing the Strengthening-of-the-Heart exercise, your heart is now bigger, stronger, and more open. In addition to repeating this practice daily for the best results, you will now learn the Open Heart Meditation, which will begin to cleanse your heart of all the negativities that have been accumulating for so many years.

Practicing the Open Heart Meditation is the best way cleanse and open our heart. Through this, we will also learn the most important part of this heart practice, which is to pray from our heart to True Source.

Now, even though I call this practice Open Heart Meditation, the type of "meditation" here is different from commonly known concepts in the sense that we are not trying to "empty" ourselves. We want to be relaxed, but we are never vacant. It's actually not good to be "gone" in whatever exercise we do. Also, we don't visualize anything, focus on our breathing, chant mantras, or move our body into poses. We are simply relying on True Source's Blessing completely. This is what we do. This is all we need.

As you know, we use the term "True Source" to refer to the Source of our true self; however, please feel free to use the terms and the words that you are familiar and comfortable with. Also, this Open Heart Meditation is not intended to replace the prayers that you say daily.

For the best results, do this meditation twice a day. First, do it in the morning so your heart is calm and light all day. Then do it again in the evening, after you have completed your daily activities, so that all excessive thoughts or burdens can be cleansed.

After doing Open Heart Meditation, you will feel peaceful, sleep better, and wake up fresh in the morning. If you don't have enough time to do this meditation twice a day, doing it once a day routinely will also give you benefits when practiced continuously for several days. You will feel your heart and your whole self become happier, more peaceful, and lighter in your daily life.

If you feel pressure on your chest during or after the prayer— or experience any other kind of emotional or physical reaction, such as laughing, crying, coughing, or soreness—this is a good sign: As the Open Heart Meditation is really a prayer asking for True Source's Blessing to remove negativities from our heart, those pressures and emotions are actually the cleansing being done by the Blessing, pushing out the negativities.

When you experience any pressures or emotional cleansing while praying, don't follow the negativities as they leave your body. All you need to do is relax and surrender more, and you will feel lighter.

After you are able to let True Source's Blessing work to remove the negativities from your heart, you may feel that there is a vacant space in your heart. This means that the negativities have been expelled and your heart is lighter. It's not empty, though, because, as the prayer says, we are asking for True Source's Blessings to replace those negativities. Thus, that vacant space actually has been filled by the Blessings, which is something very beautiful.

Let us now prepare our heart and ourselves for Open Heart Meditation. While the instructions and the prayer are written here, it is best to listen to a voice recording. You can either make the recording yourself, or listen to the Open Heart Meditation recording, available from smiletoyourheart.org.

1. Find a peaceful, quiet place to do this meditation, where you won't be distracted or interrupted.
2. Sit down and relax, keeping your spine straight without tensing yourself.
3. Place both palms on your lap, with your palms facing upward.
4. Close your eyes so that your brain is not active.
5. Relax and smile… To do this Open Heart Meditation the best way, let your whole self be here and now completely.
6. While relaxing and smiling, inhale deeply without forcing yourself, and then exhale through your mouth… Let all the burdens on your mind be expelled as you exhale. Feel and enjoy this moment when your thoughts are becoming more relaxed, as you continue to smile freely.
7. Inhale deeply, and exhale through your mouth, letting all the tension in your body be removed as you exhale. Feel your whole body as it becomes more relaxed. Enjoy

moments like this when your whole self is relaxed, and let yourself smile even more freely.

8. Inhale deeply, and exhale through the mouth, allowing all remaining thoughts and tension in your body to be removed.

9. Your body and mind are now very relaxed.

10. Smile, enjoying this moment when you are completely relaxed, body and mind.

11. From now on, breathe normally, inhaling and exhaling from the nose.

12. Now, place your fingers or one or both palms on the center of your chest where your heart is located, and smile to your heart. Do not think or try to find the exact location of your heart; just smile freely, while listening to the instructions.

13. Keep on smiling freely to your heart, with all of your feeling. Realize that you are becoming calmer. Enjoy, while continuing to smile... This is the moment when you are letting your heart become stronger.

14. Keeping your fingers or palm(s) on your chest while smiling freely to your heart and enjoying the calmness from your heart, let us now pray for True Source's Blessing, asking that the emotions in our heart be cleansed, so that our heart can open even more to True Source.

15. While praying, do not repeat the prayer lines. For the best, simply let your heart pray:

> *True Source... Please bless our heart, so that all*
> *arrogance is replaced with Your Blessings.*
> *True Source... Please bless our heart, so that all anger*
> *is replaced with Your Blessings.*

True Source… Please bless our heart, so that all
selfishness is replaced with Your Blessings.
True Source… Please bless our heart, so that all envy
and jealousy are replaced with Your Blessings.
True Source… Please bless our heart, so that all
cunningness and greediness are replaced with Your
Blessings.
True Source… Please help us to realize that our heart
is the key to our connection to You… That we must
keep our heart clean, because our connection to You is
the most important thing… Please bless and help us
to forgive others, sincerely….

16. Now, for one minute, forgive those who have done you wrong, even if they are still hurting you. Remember that your connection to True Source is the most important thing.

True Source, by forgiving those who have done us
wrong, please bless our heart so that all hatred,
grudges, resentment, dissatisfaction, and all other
negative emotions are removed from our heart, to be
replaced with Your Blessings.
True Source… Please bless and help us to realize all of
our mistakes to You, and to others. Help us so we can
regret them, and ask for forgiveness sincerely…

17. Now, for one minute, realize all of our mistakes to True Source and to others… Regret them and ask for forgiveness.

True Source, please forgive all of our mistakes to You
and to others…
Having been forgiven, let all burdens, fear, worries, and
all other negative emotions caused by those mistakes

*be cleansed from our whole heart and our whole self
to be replaced with Your Blessings.*

*True Source, please bless our heart, so all worries and
fears caused by the lack of trust in You be cleansed
and replaced with Your Blessings.*

*True Source... With the negative emotions removed
from our heart, please bless our heart to open better to
You, and to also be directed even better to You... Let
Your Blessings flow more abundantly into our heart,
so our feeling becomes stronger, so we can feel the
calmness, the peace, and the beauty of Your Blessings
even better.*

*True Source, let Your Blessings to fill our whole heart
and our whole self, so that our whole heart and our
whole self are filled with calmness and peace... So we
can rely more on Your Blessings... So we are always
within our heart, and within Your Blessings...*

*True Source, Thank You for Your Love that has removed
the negative emotions from our heart and our whole
self. Thank You for opening and directing our heart
even better to You, so that our whole heart and our
whole self are filled with Your Blessings even more...
So we can feel and enjoy the calmness, the peace, and
the beauty of Your Blessings even better.*

Thank You, True Source... Amen.

18. Keeping one or both of your palms on your chest while smiling, feel that your heart and your whole self are becoming even lighter...enjoy. Stay within this peace and calmness. This is the moment when you are within your heart. Keep on smiling and enjoying.

19. While smiling and enjoying, let yourself be pulled even deeper into the peace and calmness of the Blessings, and

dissolve even more within this peace and calmness… Feel… The more dissolved you are in this peace and calmness, the lighter and the more beautiful your feeling is. Enjoy…

20. Continuing to smile while enjoying the peace, the calmness, and the beauty of True Source's Love, slowly move your fingers, and open your eyes with a happy smile.

21. Live your daily life staying within your heart—within the peace and the calmness from True Source's Blessings.

In the next chapters, you will find more advanced heart exercises to help you open, strengthen, and use your heart even better. However, if you don't have someone guiding you, it would be best to repeat the previous exercises until you can feel the benefits before moving on. You'll know you're ready when:

- You are able to feel the light, calm, peaceful, joyful feeling from your heart when practicing the Strengthening-of-the-Heart exercise and Open Heart Meditation, and

- You can feel the calmness and happiness in your heart not only while practicing, but also in your daily life.

9

MORE ADVANCED HEART EXERCISES

You're making wonderful progress! To see, simply close your eyes, touch your heart, and smile sweetly and freely to your heart... Feel how naturally it reacts now. Realize the calm, peaceful, happy feeling radiating from your heart. Just relax and enjoy this beautiful moment.

If you are not able to experience the nice feelings from your heart yet, please continue doing the previous heart exercises before moving on. It's important you take the time to practice properly, without forcing yourself or looking for results. Just relax, smile, and enjoy strengthening your heart and the feeling from your heart.

When you're ready, we'll turn to the first of our more advanced heart exercises:

- Letting Your Heart and Feeling Become Stronger
- Realizing the Presence of True Source's Blessing within Your Heart

- Realizing That True Source's Blessing Is Working
- Letting True Source's Blessing Work

LETTING YOUR HEART AND FEELING BECOME STRONGER

In this exercise, there is a new step that will help to strengthen your heart and feeling even more. But because the first points are the same as the core Strengthening-of-the-Heart exercise—as are the basic steps in all of our heart exercises—please make sure you can do them well before you start the Letting Your Heart and Feeling Become Stronger exercise:

1. Close your eyes to reduce the activities of your brain.
2. Completely relax your body and mind.
3. Breathe in deeply through your nose, and exhale through your mouth several times to help you relax even more.
4. Touch your heart with one or more fingers.
5. Smile freely to your heart without thinking how.
6. Staying relaxed, with your eyes still closed, smile to your heart (for about one minute). When you find yourself thinking, don't follow your thoughts. Just relax and allow them to pass easily through your head.
7. Gradually, you should start experiencing an expansion in your chest area, along with feelings of calm, peace, lightness, or joy.
8. As your heart continues to expand and grow, keep on following the pleasant feeling for one minute or longer to let your heart and feeling become even stronger and deeper.

The next step must be done with your eyes closed, while staying relaxed, smiling, and touching your heart.

9. Now, let your whole feeling and your whole self be pulled into this expanding, light, calm, peaceful feeling. Realize how the more you follow and allow the pulling into the wonderful sensation, your heart and feeling are becoming stronger and deeper. Continue this process without stopping for two to three minutes.

As your heart and feeling have grown through regularly practicing the previous Strengthening-of-the-Heart exercise (corresponding to steps 1 to 8 here), your heart should react automatically. You should feel the pulling. This is why it's recommended that you continue enjoying the earlier exercises before moving on—so you can feel and receive the full benefits from these more advanced practices.

Once you are able to allow your heart to easily and naturally pull you deeper into the wonderful feeling, you can move on to the next three exercises, which should be done in sequence: The first two are actually parts of the third, which is a more complete and very beautiful practice. So for the best results, we will begin with the initial exercises in order:

- Realizing the Presence of True Source's Blessing within Your Heart
- Realizing That True Source's Blessing Is Working

Once you have properly completed and enjoyed these two exercises one by one, we can proceed to the full practice:

- Letting True Source's Blessing Work

REALIZING THE PRESENCE OF TRUE SOURCE'S BLESSING WITHIN YOUR HEART

As with every heart exercise, we start this practice by following the basic steps to strengthen our heart. Then, once we are enjoying all of the wonderful feelings from our heart, we will begin to realize the presence of True Source's Blessing within our heart:

1. Close your eyes to reduce the activities of your brain.
2. Completely relax your body and mind.
3. Breathe in deeply through your nose, and exhale through your mouth several times to help you relax even more.
4. Touch your heart with one or more fingers.
5. Smile freely to your heart without thinking how.
6. With your eyes still closed and staying relaxed, smile to your heart for about one minute. When you find yourself thinking, don't follow your thoughts; just relax, and allow them to pass easily through your head.
7. Gradually, you should start experiencing an expansion in your chest area, along with feelings of calmness, peace, lightness, or joy.
8. As your heart continues to expand and grow, keep on following your feeling one minute or longer with no observation from your brain—to let your heart and feeling become even stronger and deeper.

The next steps must be done with your eyes closed, while staying relaxed, smiling, and touching your heart.

9. Let your whole feeling and your whole self be pulled into this expanding, light, calm, peaceful feeling. Realize how the more you follow and allow the pulling into the wonderful sensation, the more your heart and feeling are becoming stronger. Continue this process without stopping for two to three minutes.
10. Now, realize that the joyful, expanding, light, calm, peaceful feeling you are experiencing is from True

Source's Blessing within your heart. Feel how your heart and feeling react as soon as you realize this. Keep on following the shifts in your feeling, which will strengthen your heart even more.

11. Now, for understanding, stop realizing that the joyful feeling is from the presence of True Source's Blessing within your heart. Regard this beautiful sensation as just a feeling from your heart instead of from True Source's Blessing. Recognize how the radiating feeling from your heart is diminishing.

12. Realize again that the joyful feeling in your heart is from True Source's Blessing. Feel the changes in your heart and feeling, and follow the changes as they grow and expand.

13. Repeat steps 11 and 12 two to three times, recognizing the shifts in your feeling. As you complete the final step, follow the changes in your feeling even farther and deeper. You should experience a radiating, more joyful and beautiful feeling within your heart. Stay relaxed and keep on smiling sweetly and freely to your heart for another two to three minutes.

As with the Letting Your Heart and Feeling Become Stronger exercise, to realize that the beautiful, joyful feeling is from True Source's Blessing, simply let your whole self be pulled into the expanding, light, calm, peaceful feeling. Don't try to become aware of or feel anything; just let your heart do it.

REALIZING THAT TRUE SOURCE'S BLESSING IS WORKING

Once you are able to allow your heart and feeling to easily and beautifully expand with the realization of True Source's

Blessing within your heart, you're ready to move on to the next practice.

So, whenever you feel it's time, you can start the following exercise, Realizing That True Source's Blessing Is Working:

1. Close your eyes to reduce the activities of your brain.
2. Completely relax your body and mind.
3. Breathe in deeply through your nose, and exhale through your mouth several times to help you relax even more.
4. Touch your heart with one or more fingers.
5. Smile freely to your heart without thinking how.
6. With your eyes still closed and staying relaxed, smile to your heart (for about one minute). When you find yourself thinking, don't follow your thoughts: Just relax, and allow them to pass easily through your head.
7. Gradually, you should start experiencing an expansion in your chest area, along with feelings of calmness, peace, lightness, or joy.
8. As your heart continues to expand and grow, keep on following the pleasant feeling for one minute or longer to let your heart and feeling become even stronger and deeper.

The next steps must be done with your eyes closed, while staying relaxed, smiling, and touching your heart.

9. Let your whole feeling and your whole self be pulled into this expanding, light, calm, peaceful feeling. Recognize how the more you follow and allow the pulling into the wonderful sensation, your heart and feeling are becoming stronger. Continue this process without stopping for two to three minutes.
10. Realize that the joyful, expanding, light, calm, peaceful feeling you are experiencing is from True Source's Bless-

ing within your heart. Feel how your heart and feeling react as soon as you realize this. Keep following the shifts in your feeling to strengthen your heart even more.

11. Also realize that True Source's Blessing within your heart is helping you in so many ways. Feel clearly how your already-strengthened feeling is becoming even deeper and more beautiful.

12. Now, for understanding, stop realizing that True Source's Blessing is working within your heart. Recognize how your feeling that was strengthened by the realization now weakens, and the way in which the feeling radiates also diminishes.

13. Realize again how True Source's Blessing within your heart is helping your heart, in everything. Recognize how your feeling is becoming strong again, and begins to radiate so wonderfully. Follow the changes in your feeling to allow it to grow and strengthen further.

14. Repeat Steps 12 and 13 several times until your feeling is strong and free. Then, continue following the changes in your feeling while staying relaxed and smiling sweetly and freely to your heart for another two to three minutes.

We include the "realize / don't realize" variation to help us understand and follow our feeling more naturally. After completing this exercise, your heart will certainly become stronger— so please do the practice properly, though you may not want to let the feeling fade.

LETTING TRUE SOURCE'S BLESSING WORK

This heart exercise is a more complete meditation that includes the previous two exercises. When you do your daily practice, just follow this Letting True Source's Blessing Work exercise:

1. Close your eyes to reduce the activities of your brain.
2. Completely relax your body and mind, so that your whole self is quiet.
3. Breathe in deeply through your nose, and exhale through your mouth several times to help you relax even more.
4. Touch your heart with one or more fingers.
5. Smile freely to your heart without thinking how.
6. With your eyes still closed and staying relaxed, smile to your heart (for about one minute). When you find yourself thinking, don't follow your thoughts. Just relax and allow them to pass easily through your head.
7. Gradually, you should start experiencing an expansion in your chest area, along with feelings of calmness, peace, lightness, or joy.
8. As your heart continues to expand and grow, keep on following your feeling for one minute or longer, with no observation from your brain to let your heart and feeling become even stronger and deeper.

The next steps must be done with your eyes closed, while staying relaxed, smiling, and touching your heart.

9. Let your whole feeling and your whole self be pulled into this expanding light, calm, peaceful feeling. Realize how the more you follow and allow the pulling into the wonderful sensation, your heart and feeling are becoming stronger. Continue this process without stopping for two to three minutes.
10. Realize that the joyful, expanding, light, calm, peaceful feeling you are experiencing is from True Source's Blessing within your heart. Feel how your heart and feeling react as soon as you realize this. Keep on following the shifts in your feeling to strengthen your heart even more.

11. Also realize that True Source's Blessing within your heart is helping your heart in everything. Feel clearly how your already strengthened feeling is becoming even deeper and more beautiful.

12. Let True Source's Blessing work. Realize how the joyful feeling within your heart, which is from True Source's Blessing, radiates farther, stronger, and freer.

13. Now, for understanding, do not let True Source's Blessing work for a moment. Recognize how the radiating feeling is blocked.

14. Let True Source's Blessing work again. As soon as you feel True Source's Blessing radiate far and free, let it radiate even farther, more beautifully and expansively, while continuing to smile sweetly and freely.

15. Repeat Steps 13 and 14 two to three times. Then keep on letting True Source's Blessing radiate far and free, without any limit, while staying relaxed and smiling sweetly and freely.

> When you can feel the changes in your feeling
> as you do the exercises presented in this chapter,
> it means your heart has become stronger.

When your heart is strong enough that it allows you to follow the changes in your feeling, you can rely on True Source's Blessing within your heart to:

- Pray
- Smile
- Interact with others
- Do your daily activities

These steps will be discussed in Chapter 12: Improving Our Connection to True Source and in Chapter 13: Heart in Our Daily Life. To help prepare you for these important heart exercises, the next two chapters will focus on information and guidelines to further improve the quality of your heart exercises—allowing you to relax better, smile more freely, and enjoy your practices even more deeply.

10

KEYS IN STRENGTHENING YOUR HEART & FEELING

In teaching and guiding participants at Open Heart Workshops and other heart classes, I notice that many students make some progress as they repeat the heart exercises. However, there are some who, even though they can feel the expanding, calm, light, joyful feeling every time they practice, don't progress as well as they might.

The main reason is that when doing the heart exercises, as soon as these students start feeling something, they hold themselves back. They simply stay in that nice feeling, and don't allow True Source's Blessing to help pull them deeper and strengthen their heart more.

Being able to feel the light, calm, peaceful, joyful feeling is wonderful, and doing the exercises regularly and properly can make it even more wonderful.

By analogy, if you're just learning to play basketball, and you happen to make a few hoops in a row while shooting around by yourself, you wouldn't go home thinking you're a good basketball player. Not yet, anyway.

Instead, you would want to keep practicing through a range of different exercises, drills, and game scenarios, alongside and against skillful and experienced players. As a result, you would begin to develop a stronger, more detailed and nuanced sense of what it actually means to be a good basketball player: identifying where and how you can continue to grow and improve. Even the best pro athletes, when interviewed, report that the sport continues to be challenging and interesting for them because there is always a higher level they can take their game to.

With the heart exercises, in this way, you want to let True Source's Blessing keep on helping you to strengthen your heart and feeling even more.

IMPROVING THE STARTING STEPS

Of the four key steps in strengthening the heart—relaxing, closing your eyes, touching your heart, and smiling to your heart—there is not much we can improve on in closing our eyes and touching our heart, obviously. However, there is quite a lot we can do to help us better relax and smile to our heart.

Please remember, though, that any effort on your part to "do better" will only hold you back. We are simply improving our technique to allow us to enjoy more easily and completely. To make the best progress, just follow the steps properly.

Relaxing

Even though you may feel that you are already relaxed while practicing, being truly relaxed is actually quite deep. To help you understand and let go more, try this: Without looking or putting in extra thought, realize which parts of your body are tense or not completely relaxed at this moment. Now, without any effort, simply allow those parts to relax... Feel the difference? Were you aware that you were holding in those places?

When you do the heart exercises, you can practice this technique to help you relax better. Be careful not to overdo it, though, as you can become too busy and preoccupied trying to make yourself relax more—which, of course, has the opposite effect.

> Whenever you read or hear the instruction to "relax," simply let go of your thoughts and all tension in your body without rushing.

Smiling to Your Heart

When smiling while doing the heart exercises, always smile sweetly and freely to your heart. You will realize how, by smiling sweeter and freer, your feeling becomes stronger and even more joyful.

At the same time, please remember that improving the quality of your smile here does not mean that you exaggerate or force your physical smile. Doing so will only uncomfortably tighten your facial muscles and cause you to become less relaxed and eventually tired.

In smiling—especially in smiling sweetly and freely—you need to rely on your heart and the feeling from your heart. But just smiling physically helps a great deal. If you don't move your lips, for sure you are holding back and not allowing the best.

> Always smile sweetly and freely to your heart
> to strengthen your feeling.

THE NEXT KEY STEP:
FOLLOW YOUR FEELING

Even if you feel that your heart exercises are already so enjoyable and that you're getting wonderful results, the next key step in improving the quality of your practices is to follow your feeling continuously.

We want to open our heart completely to True Source. *Completely* means boundlessly, without limits. No matter how open you feel your heart is, and however beautiful the light, calm, peaceful, joyous feeling you have experienced, there is still much room to grow.

The best way to open your heart is simply to always follow your feeling without stopping, to let the Blessings do the most wonderful things to your heart and your feeling.

Relaxing completely, smiling sweetly and freely, and following your feeling continuously are the foundation for all the heart practices. Know these steps well, and improve upon them with each exercise you do.

At every level of heart practices, these basic, key steps never diminish in importance. So please do the best you can, never limiting yourself, to get the best results.

> Relaxing completely, smiling sweetly and freely,
> and following your feeling continuously are the
> foundation for all the heart practices.

TRUE SOURCE'S BLESSING IS AT WORK

As you have probably experienced for yourself, when our brain is active or trying to control the process while doing heart exercises, we don't get very good results. Any effort from the mind, though well-intentioned, will only block our heart and feeling.

Instead, the right and natural method, as you have practiced, is to relax, smile to your heart, and enjoy the nice, pleasant feeling—which strengthens your heart and feeling in the most wonderful and easy way.

The most important realization, which makes the "technical" details behind improving the quality of your heart exercises even possible, is that True Source's Blessing is at work in all of this. If you think that your own heart is able to cleanse, open, and strengthen itself, you can try the following experiment.

For those of you who have already realized True Source's Blessing working on you while doing the heart practices, I do not recommend that you try this exercise.

1. Close your eyes to reduce the activities of your brain.
2. Completely relax your body and mind so that your whole self is quiet.
3. Breathe in deeply through your nose, and exhale through your mouth several times to help you relax even more.
4. Touch your heart with one or more fingers.
5. Smile freely to your heart without thinking how.
6. With your eyes still closed and staying relaxed, smile to your heart (for about one minute). When you find yourself thinking, don't follow your thoughts. Just relax, and allow them to pass through your head.
7. Gradually, you should start experiencing an expansion in your chest area, along with feelings of calmness, peace, lightness, or joy.

8. Intend to see that all of these nice feelings are there simply as a result of your own heart and feeling, without the help of True Source's Blessing. Realize how your feeling becomes heavy or pressured with this perception. This is because you are not letting True Source's Blessing help you, and your own heart is protesting.

9. Now, realize that all the wonderful and beautiful things happening to your heart are from True Source's Blessing. Realize, too, that the expanding, light, calm, peaceful, joyful feeling is also from True Source's Love and Blessing within your heart. Feel how True Source's Blessing starts working again, and all of the nice feelings return.

While you don't want to repeat it, this small exercise should help you better understand how True Source's Blessing is always at work...when we allow it to be.

11

OPENING OUR HEART & OUR BRAIN BLOCKING OUR HEART: A VISUAL STORY

Now that you have experienced the wonderful feelings from the heart practices, looking at some simple illustrations that show the condition of the heart after doing each exercise will help you to better understand the process of opening your heart and letting True Source's Blessing work.

Of course, since the state of one person's heart is different from another's, the drawings and explanations presented here give only a general idea of how each exercise benefits your heart and helps it to grow. But the visual learning will complement your realizations from the reading, certainly.

Following this discussion, we will cover several more illustrations depicting how our brain can block our heart and hold it back from opening and radiating more. Knowing the process of how your brain obstructs your heart will help you to recognize when it happens during the exercises and allow you to do your heart practices better and more joyfully.

Finally, we'll also go over some reminders on how to do the heart exercises properly. Not that you've forgotten already; just a little reinforcement!

STRENGTHENING-OF-THE-HEART EXERCISE

When the Strengthening-of-the-Heart exercise is done properly, your heart begins to open a little, and True Source's Blessing starts radiating. If your feeling is strong and does not block True Source's Blessing at all, you should start feeling the expanding, light, calm, peaceful, joyful feeling.

If you still cannot feel the nice feeling from your heart after doing this exercise ten or more times, please carefully read the "Your Brain Blocking Your Heart" section later in this chapter, as this is the likely cause.

Figure 4a shows the condition of your heart after doing the Strengthening-of-the-Heart exercise several times. Your heart should already be open, and True Source's Blessing has begun to radiate. If your brain is still strong, however, it will block your heart from expanding (shown by the circle around the opened area of your heart in the illustration). Conversely, if your brain is relaxed and not disrupting your feeling, your heart would naturally open more on its own.

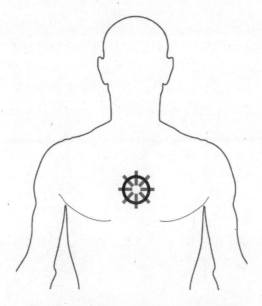

Figure 4a. Condition of your heart after doing
Strengthening-of-the-Heart exercise several times

OPEN HEART MEDITATION

After doing Open Heart Meditation several times, the condition of your heart typically improves quite a lot:

- Your heart opens more.
- True Source's Blessing radiates more brightly.
- True Source's Blessing fills your heart.

The negativities on the surface of your heart also start to be removed, so you can enjoy the Blessing better.

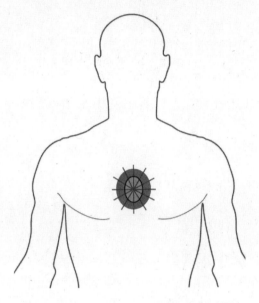

Figure 4b. Condition of your heart after doing
Open Heart Meditation several times

LETTING YOUR HEART AND
FEELING BECOME STRONGER

Here, the attention from your brain toward your heart has lessened. As a result, your brain doesn't block or limit your heart as much anymore. The feeling from your heart is also becoming stronger, as True Source's Blessing grows brighter and stronger, and radiates even more beautifully.

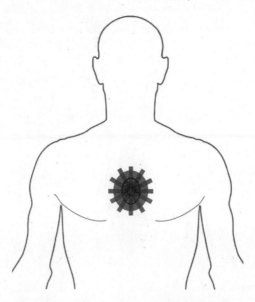

Figure 4c. Condition of your heart when you are
letting your heart and feeling become stronger

REALIZING THE PRESENCE OF TRUE SOURCE'S BLESSING WITHIN YOUR HEART

By realizing the presence of True Source's Blessing within your heart, you are letting the Blessing become stronger, able to do many more wonderful things for your whole heart and self. True Source's Blessing also radiates wider, filling the area of your heart that has been opened, as well as the area around your heart.

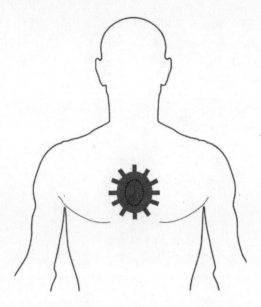

Figure 4d. Condition of your heart when you realize the presence
of True Source's Blessing within your heart

REALIZING THAT TRUE SOURCE'S BLESSING IS WORKING

When we realize that True Source's Blessing within our heart is working, we let the Blessing radiate even stronger, wider, and fuller. Our feeling and experience of the Blessing is also deeper and more joyful, as True Source is able to cleanse many more impurities from our heart, as well as help us to relax and smile even better.

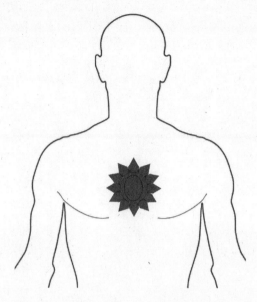

*Figure 4e. Condition of your heart when you realize
True Source's Blessing within your heart is working*

LETTING TRUE SOURCE'S BLESSING WORK

By letting True Source's Blessing within your heart work, you are allowing the Blessing to cleanse, open, and direct your heart better and more completely to True Source. The Blessing, when it is free to help you the best, is also doing so many other wonderful things to your whole heart and whole being, radiating farther, stronger, and brighter to purify and remove all negativities. There is no limit to what True Source wants to give.

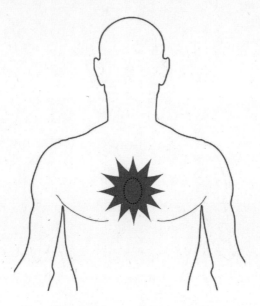

*Figure 4f. Condition of your heart when you are
letting True Source's Blessing work*

Hopefully, seeing a visual of how your heart grows and expands with each of the exercises has helped you to better understand the process of opening your heart for True Source, and why each step is so important.

In addition to using illustrations to understand better about how your heart opens, looking at the different ways your brain can block your heart will help you too.

YOUR BRAIN BLOCKING YOUR HEART

As our brain is very busy, involved in many different activities that interfere with us accepting True Source's Blessing, it is important that you understand each of the different ways your brain can block your heart. This will help you to better recognize what your brain is doing, and allow you let go more easily.

So let's discuss the following four common scenarios, where your brain is:

1. Putting in effort
2. Observing your heart
3. Watching the ongoing process
4. Discrediting your heart

1. YOUR BRAIN PUTTING IN EFFORT

Once you have practiced all of the exercises presented in this book, the condition of your heart should be as shown in Figure 4f., after finishing the Letting True Source's Blessing Work exercise. We'll now review this drawing again in Figure 5, to better understand the effect on your heart when your brain is active.

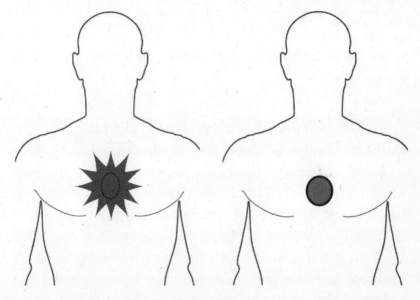

Figure 5. Side-by-side comparison of Letting True Source's Blessing Work and your brain putting in effort

Looking at Figure 5 on the left, when True Source's Blessing is working, you can see how open your heart is. The dashes form a circle illustrating the border of your heart; yet the Blessing radiates well beyond the opened area of your heart.

The illustration to the right, on the other hand, shows the condition of your heart when your brain is putting in effort—trying to grow the feeling from your heart, or perhaps even attempting to direct the Blessing. Not only does this prevent True Source's Blessing from radiating beyond the border of your heart, but it also creates a wall much thicker than the normal border of your heart.

So the stronger and the more often your brain exerts effort in any process of opening your heart, the more pressure is created and put upon your heart. Continuously recognize when this may be happening—for instance, when you become aware of your thoughts, or find that the nice feelings from your heart begin to diminish—and let it remind you to relax better and enjoy even more.

2. YOUR BRAIN OBSERVING YOUR HEART

Our brain also has a habit of always wanting to know what's going on around us. In everyday life, of course, this generally turns out to be a useful and necessary tendency. In heart practices, though, this can be a big limitation.

When we observe our heart with our brain—trying to inspect the Blessing, the nice feelings, or the negativities being cleansed—we place pressure on our heart from above.

While not as restrictive as when our brain puts in actual effort, when we observe our heart, we nonetheless limit the benefits we can receive by blocking the Blessing from radiating completely.

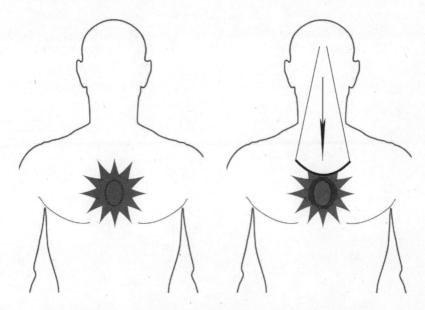

Figure 6. Side-by-side comparison of Letting True Source's Blessing Work and your brain observing your heart

Looking at Figure 6, you can see how observation places an upward border on your heart, reducing its overall ability to let True Source's Blessing radiate far and free. Although less limiting than the thick wall seen in Figure 5, we of course don't want to impose any boundaries at all on what the Blessing can do for us.

3. YOUR BRAIN WATCHING THE ONGOING PROCESS

Even if you are already able to let your brain relax well, and aren't putting in any effort or observing your heart (at least most of the time), your brain still wants to get involved by watching the ongoing process of True Source's Blessing working.

When your brain tries to observe the wonderful things happening to your heart, it actually blocks the cleansing, opening,

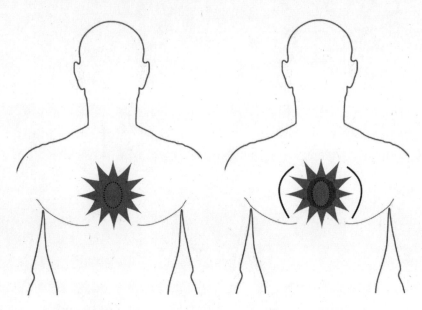

Figure 7. Side-by-side comparison of Letting True Source's Blessing Work and your brain observing the ongoing process

and strengthening of your heart done by True Source's Blessing—which puts pressure on your heart from the sides, as shown in Figure 7.

Again, watching the process is not as limiting as actively putting in effort. However, both represent "doing" on your part, which blocks the Blessing from working completely.

YOUR BRAIN DISCREDITING YOUR HEART

For the first three ways we've discussed so far in which your brain can block your heart, it has been a matter of effort and observation limiting how well True Source's Blessing can work on your heart.

Your brain discrediting your heart, on the other hand, is more related to how often and how completely you follow your thoughts and their effects.

As your heart begins the process of opening and becoming strong, it is quite common to question or doubt what you experience. For example, when you start feeling that expanding, light, calm, peaceful, joyous feeling, your brain is thinking and wondering, "Is this it?" or "Am I doing it right?" or "Is that all?" You may also sometimes become hesitant that the wonderful feelings are really from True Source's Blessing within your heart.

Doubt is a lever that your brain uses in an attempt to stay in control, not wanting to relinquish authority to the heart. This makes you look for sensations other than what you are feeling, and for reasons other than why you are feeling them. As a result, misgivings from your brain keep you busy searching and looking and trying—preventing you from recognizing moments when you are already doing the heart exercises properly, and from fully enjoying the feeling from your heart.

HOW IT IS SUPPOSED TO BE

Now that we know what to do—and what not to do—in practicing our heart exercises properly, let's review and remember the following key points once more before moving on:

- You cannot open your heart on your own. Only True Source's Blessing can cleanse, open, and strengthen your heart.
- In doing your heart exercises, remember to always stay relaxed, touch your heart, and keep on smiling sweetly and freely.

- When you have thoughts, just relax more and smile more while allowing your thoughts to pass easily through your head.
- As soon as you start experiencing the nice feeling from your heart, don't think, don't pay attention to it or observe what's happening; just enjoy that wonderful feeling, letting it grow bigger and stronger as you stay relaxed and smiling freely.
- When you follow and enjoy the expanding, light, calm, peaceful, joyous feeling, you are letting True Source's Blessing help you in the best way possible.

12

IMPROVING OUR CONNECTION TO TRUE SOURCE

"In prayer, it is better to have a heart without words than words without a heart."

~ JOHN BUNYAN, 1628–1688

Where Is God?
I tried to find Him on the Christian cross, but He was not there.

I went to the temple of the Hindus and to the old pagodas, but I could not find a trace of Him anywhere.

I searched on the mountains and in the valleys, but neither in the heights nor in the depths was I able to find Him.

I went to the Kaaba in Mecca, but He was not there either.

I questioned the scholars and philosophers, but He was beyond their understanding.

I then looked into my heart, and it was there where He
dwelled that I saw Him; He was nowhere else to be found.

~ JALALUDDIN RUMI, 1207–1273

The quote from John Bunyan and the poem from Jalaluddin Rumi clearly remind us that the importance of the heart has been known for many centuries, how the heart is our real connection to True Source. It is only our heart—where the spark of the Divine Source, our true self, resides—that can be connected to and communicate with the Creator of all existence, including our own.

Our heart can understand divinity on a level much deeper than our brain can; and even then, our heart can't know the complete and full truth. Rather, it is only the deepest part of our heart—its core, or our Inner Heart—that can realize True Source's Will (which is beyond the scope of this book). Using our heart and Inner Heart, we have a much deeper and wider perspective, and can in fact grasp the essence of an idea or a belief.

Renowned 17th-century philosopher and mathematician Blaise Pascal actually captured the concept quite succinctly, remarking, "The heart has its reasons, of which reason knows nothing."

So now that you know more about the importance of your heart—realizing and feeling for yourself, in doing the exercises, that your heart is the key connection to True Source— how would you like to continue using your heart to improve your connection and make it more beautiful?

HOW THE HEART EXERCISES HELP IMPROVE YOUR CONNECTION TO TRUE SOURCE

By doing the heart exercises presented so far, you have let True Source's Blessing cleanse, open, and strengthen your heart. And at the same time, each and every practice improves your connection to True Source, as you learn to receive and accept the Blessing better and better. The exercises also help you to surrender more completely to True Source, as well as pray from your heart, be grateful from your heart, and surrender all of your problems and burdens to True Source from your heart.

Have you ever heard people say that our heart is deeper than the ocean? In reality, it's much deeper than even that. So in using our heart to surrender better, to pray, to be grateful, and to give over our problems and burdens to True Source, we are moving to a deeper part of our heart than in doing the previous exercises. Those were just the beginning steps, the building blocks, for more advanced practices, which we'll begin to discuss now.

SURRENDERING TO TRUE SOURCE

When we surrender to True Source, we are letting True Source's Blessing work on us in the best way. Surrendering means we allow the Blessing to help, guide, and protect us—giving us what's best according to True Source's Will.

But talking about surrendering to True Source or even wanting to surrender does not mean that we are already able to surrender properly to True Source. In fact, there is often quite some distance between the intention and the action.

Of course, all of the heart exercises offered here are based on surrendering to True Source. Letting the Blessings work on our heart and our feeling while we simply relax, smile, and enjoy *is* surrendering to True Source in practice. Yet there are still deeper understandings.

We know that we are not able to open our own heart—as only True Source's Blessing can do it—and that the expanding, light, calm, peaceful, joyous feeling in our heart comes from True Source's Blessing. So in opening our heart by doing the exercises and enjoying the feeling, we are in fact realizing that True Source's Blessing is really at work. When practicing with this understanding, you are taking the first actual step in surrendering to True Source.

Now that you have learned a number of natural heart exercises that can help you surrender properly from your heart, it is simply a matter of using these techniques the right way: moving beyond just saying you want to surrender to doing it in reality, every time you practice.

PRAYING TO TRUE SOURCE USING YOUR HEART

Even though your heart has opened and been strengthened by doing the heart exercises, it is only to a certain extent. The real growth and advancement, instead, is in the *application* of what you have experienced and learned.

Using your heart fully means doing your best at all times, both in praying and in your daily life. You achieve this by drawing on the great progress you've made with the heart practices, and then letting the results guide you to the proper heart condition in each of your activities.

Hopefully, you have already started to experience the benefits in your everyday routine: feeling lighter, happier, and less troubled as a result of opening and strengthening your heart. You should also have now realized the calmness, peace, and joy from praying with a stronger and more open heart, as compared to using only your brain. Some of you, in fact, may be feeling these differences quite clearly, not only in times of devotion, but consistently as you go about your day.

At this stage, however, you will likely still find it easier to use your heart better when praying than in doing your daily activities—which, of course, requires heavy use of the brain. So while this is very deep and practiced at the highest levels, I will now give you the first steps to pray to True Source using your heart.

As you begin to use your heart properly and completely in praying, let your heart call out to True Source as shown:

1. Close your eyes to reduce the activities of your brain.
2. Completely relax your body and mind.
3. Breathe in deeply through your nose, and exhale through your mouth several times to help you relax even more.
4. Touch your heart with one or more fingers.
5. Smile freely to your heart without thinking how.
6. With your eyes still closed and staying relaxed, smile to your heart (for about one minute). When you find yourself thinking, don't follow your thoughts. Just relax, and allow them to pass through your head.
7. Gradually, you should start experiencing an expansion in your chest area, along with feelings of calmness, peacefulness, lightness, or joy.
8. When you feel any of the nice feelings, it's a wonderful indication that your heart is starting to work. Just follow

your feeling without observing with your brain to let your heart and feeling become stronger.

9. While continuing to follow the expanding, calm, peaceful, joyous feeling, let your heart call out to the Creator, True Source, without any words. As you do, you should feel an expansion or a beautiful feeling in your heart that is moving upward. This is your prayer from your heart to True Source. Enjoy the beauty of praying from your heart to True Source.

10. Repeat several times so that you can truly enjoy praying from your heart.

If you are already able to call out to True Source using your heart well, you can start praying without words; what's important is that you let your heart continue praying properly, without rushing.

Remembering, as always, that the key connection to True Source is your heart—not expressions from your brain—you want to let your heart pray to True Source for long enough to really follow your feeling, and enjoy the beauty and meaning of praying to True Source from your heart.

Once you are able to use your heart the best you can in praying, the next step is to use your heart this well in your daily life: experiencing the benefits of an opened and strengthened heart as you commute, work, run errands, interact with others, and so on. Now, it's certainly much easier to be in your heart when you are sitting in quiet meditation, focusing on nothing but enjoying; yet the heart is meant to be used every moment of our lives. The wonderful feelings from your heart can be enjoyed in all situations, even deeper and stronger.

The good news is that our heart is very special, and it is not difficult to fully use our heart no matter where we are or what we're doing. We'll revisit this point at greater length in the following chapter, when we discuss using our heart better in everyday life.

BEING GRATEFUL TO TRUE SOURCE

Being grateful is an important key to improving our relationship with True Source. In moments when we are grateful from our heart, we can feel the beauty of being grateful to our Creator, the Most Loving Divine Source, who always gives what is best for us.

When our hearts are open and we surrender to True Source with gratitude, we also embrace True Source's Blessings to help us, which wonderfully improves our connection to True Source.

We can easily start this process by becoming more aware, and being grateful for simple things in life that we may have taken for granted, such as:

- Our ability to breathe.
- A beautiful morning.
- Time spent with loved ones.
- The talents and strengths we have and use.
- Life events we learned and grew from.
- Every matter we can be grateful of.

Again, by being grateful, the attitude of our heart will begin to improve—which, in turn, helps strengthen our connection to and relationship with True Source. It is a beautiful cycle that not only makes our daily lives more joyful and fulfilling, but results in real spiritual progress.

SURRENDERING PROBLEMS AND BURDENS TO TRUE SOURCE

Surrendering your problems and burdens to True Source is also quite deep, and so very beautiful. Once you know how to give your troubles over to True Source by using your heart, not only will you feel lighter and more peaceful, but your connection to True Source will also improve wonderfully.

The way of surrendering problems and burdens to True Source is similar to praying without words from your heart—where the key is simply to let your heart do it, without any thought, interference, or effort.

Surrendering your problems and burdens to True Source, however, does not mean that you don't take active steps to address the issues causing concern in your life. It means that you allow True Source to give you the best help and guidance possible, both in resolving the situations and letting go of your worries.

13

HEART IN
OUR DAILY LIFE

All you have learned about the heart and all that you have practiced in this book are just the beginning steps in a beautiful journey of opening, strengthening, and using your heart. And because your heart is the key connection to True Source, any improvement in your heart and feeling automatically improves your relationship with True Source.

So please use all the learnings and results from these beginning steps as well as you can before moving on to the more advanced heart practices. To get the best results and make the most progress, really remember to:

- Relax.
- Smile sweetly and freely.
- Feel and follow the expanding, calm, peaceful, joyful feeling.

While you can't always close your eyes or touch your heart, any time you do these three things properly, you are using your heart quite well. The key difference between doing the heart exercises and using your heart in your daily life is that when you do your heart exercises, you smile sweetly and freely to your heart—while in your daily life, you are letting your heart smile sweetly and freely to others.

Once we're in the practice of using our heart at all times, our life will be filled with True Source's Blessing, and everything becomes so much more beautiful. This is the time to start taking the actual steps forward, opening and using our heart as often as possible.

So let's look at the suggested daily heart exercises you can already do, both in quiet meditation and in your daily life.

DAILY HEART PRACTICES

Allocate some time in your daily life to do the heart practices to let True Source's Blessing work on you more completely:

- Practice Open Heart Meditation.
- Do the Letting True Source's Blessing Work exercise.
- Pray to True Source Using Your Heart, letting it open for and be directed to True Source.
- Surrender to True Source as often as possible, using your heart maximally.
- Be Grateful to True Source for all of the wonderful Gifts of Love, including those we are not aware of, by using your heart maximally.

Realizing better how very deep our heart is, in the next level you will learn to let True Source's Blessing actually bring you into your heart—where you can interact with others, wherever you are and whoever you are with, while letting the Blessing radiate from your heart for all beings. Moments when you do this are moments when you are being a beautiful instrument for True Source. Being an instrument of True Source means you are letting the Blessing radiate from your toward others according to True Source's Will.

Regarding your practices, continue doing the heart exercises outlined here until you can feel and enjoy your heart and your feeling, as well as experience the benefits in your daily life. If you become stuck or questions arise, there is always support from experienced "heart alumni."

It is a great privilege and joy to help others open and strengthen their hearts, so please don't hesitate to reach out to a coordinator in your area. (Contact information is available in Appendix A). While enjoying True Source's Blessing is a gift, to share the Blessing with others is even more beautiful.

And as you've already begun to enjoy the benefits of opening and strengthening your heart, when you learn to let True Source's Blessing bring you into your heart—and then stay within the Blessing that radiates from inside your heart—everything becomes exponentially more beautiful.

BENEFITS OF USING THE HEART AT YOUR WORKPLACE

For many of us, a big portion of the waking time in our daily life is spent working. In fact, with the number of hours per day we put in just to work—and given the number of years in our lives that a job or career adds up to—to not use our heart at work would be a huge missed opportunity.

So when you are in your business or office environment, you can and should continue to use your heart. In fact, this is one of the most important times to do so for a number of reasons.

First, the peace and joy within your heart will help guide you to greater professional fulfillment, no matter the circumstances: Even in a very stressful or difficult workplace, by staying focused on following the good feeling radiating from your heart, you will be much less susceptible to negative influences and better able to enjoy your work on a much deeper level.

By sharing the peace and calmness of True Source's Blessing with everyone at your workplace—by letting your heart smile to theirs and radiating the Blessing—you will not only start to appreciate your work more, but also begin to make a real difference in the lives of others. Plus the heart doesn't just help us relax and enjoy our work more; it actually improves our decision making.

HEART: BEYOND OUR BRAIN, BEYOND OUR INTUITION

The successful decisions and innovative ideas of business-people normally arise from good analysis and intuition. The brain, of course, handles the analytical part; but intuition, often the source of "insight," is actually the result of a good connection with the soul—the intermediate consciousness between our brain consciousness and our true self consciousness (i.e., our heart). And while our soul can know a lot of things, it still can't compare to the knowledge from our heart.

Our true self consciousness, through our heart, knows so much more than our soul and so much more than our brain—even if we have the smartest brain around. Why? Because our heart is the key connection to True Source, who can guide us perfectly in all of our decisions, from big to small.

But this isn't just about doing better in business. What's more important to remember is that because our heart is the key connection to True Source, every time we use our heart, we are letting True Source's Blessing help us in so many different ways, including improving our connection to True Source.

By using our heart, our Inner Heart (the spark of True Source) becomes more active. Because our Inner Heart knows True Source's Will, it means we are doing what True Source wants us to do when we follow our heart / Inner Heart. To live our life for True Source by following our Inner Heart is a joy.

So, knowing that our heart is beyond our brain and beyond our intuition, we should use our heart in making decisions—including business decisions—because we now realize that the real purpose is to get closer to True Source.

BURDENS TURNING INTO JOY

Work is one aspect of our lives where we can really demonstrate our talents and capabilities, which should obviously be an enjoyable process. But at many points along the path, our job often fills up with worries, stress, and dissatisfaction.

Besides receiving assignments and responsibilities that we feel are too much or perhaps "below us," this frustration can stem from the behaviors and attitudes of our colleagues, our supervisors, our customers, and so on. It's to the point where many people, when they think about work, immediately become anxious and upset. At its core, this is a form of resistance. And whether we see it or not, this resistance creates pressures and burdens that negatively affect our work performance.

But by opening and using our heart at our workplace, not only will we begin to shed our negative attitudes and perceptions, but our burdens will slowly turn into joy as we find meaning in what we do.

DEVELOPING YOUR HEART AND SPIRITUAL QUOTIENT (HSQ) AT WORK

In response to increased employee turnover and performance issues, companies in the mid 1990s began to look at how our "emotional intelligence" matched with our IQ—the interplay of which affects how well we balance our reason and our interpersonal skills. For instance, a very intelligent but emotionally unstable worker will often suffer from poor relations with employees and customers, and frequently not have a clear head (never mind heart!) to make good business decisions.

Out of this research came a new measurement, Emotional Quotient (EQ), which tells about our tendency toward self-motivation, empathy, altruism, and other adaptive traits. EQ, in many workplaces, began to supplement, and in some cases replace, IQ-based evaluation systems.

But still missing from the picture was how our spiritual awareness impacts the way we deal with colleagues and clients, as well as how we perceive the deeper purpose of our job in the context of our life. It was out of this gap that the burgeoning areas of "Spiritual Quotient" (SQ) and "spiritual companies" (along with several variations of these two terms) began to gain traction in recent business seminars and articles.

And while most U.S. companies have yet to formally adopt such measures, you can start to develop your own Heart and Spiritual Quotient (HSQ), remembering that this is about using our professional life to rely on our heart and grow closer to True Source.

Through this perspective, we begin to see that we're being given exactly what we need in our work. Becoming conscious of this, our job becomes an interesting and joyful challenge—as the same, once-boring or aggravating activities slowly turn into meaningful encounters and experiences. We start to feel that we're doing something good not only for ourselves and our family, but for others and the community at large.

Realizing that our profession ultimately helps us grow closer to True Source, we also naturally become more responsible with projects, as well as more conscientious about our interactions with colleagues, subordinates, and supervisors. We begin to enjoy our work on a much deeper level, find it easier to do, reach our goals more effectively, and smile with sincerity as we go about our day. We also become more grateful to True Source for this opportunity to use our heart in leading, interacting with, and serving others.

LEADING, INTERACTING, AND SERVING FROM THE HEART

No matter your role, there are wonderful opportunities to use and boost your HSQ at work.

If you are in the position of managing others, when you use your heart in leading, you will be able to more easily understand your team's needs and bring out the best strengths and attributes in each individual team member. People will feel supported, cared for, and more willing and eager to put forth the kind of effort that results in a meaningful impact on your business and goals.

Those who work with customers or internal teams will likewise discover how using the heart makes the job easier, as encounters with others become happier, lighter, and more positive. In serving from the heart, help is given with much more sincerity and less reluctance, and an overall sense of meaning and joy fills the day.

HOW HSQ BENEFITS COMPANIES

A good HSQ, by continuation, improves business-to-business relations with suppliers and customers—because these, of course, also come down to people-to-people interactions. If everyone in the organization has the proper HSQ attitude and realization, it will begin to re-orient the company away from bottom-line decisions that negatively impact employees and focus on quick profits, and toward a longer-term global and community consciousness.

Far from a fiscally impractical decision, you can already see early results with certain firms who have embraced a "green" approach to business and the positive customer response it has generated. And this is just one aspect of a shift to more environmental responsibility. Just think if the entire organization were to adopt a heart-centered operating philosophy.

If you manage employee programs, or would like to introduce your human resources department to HSQ, information on training programs offered by Padmacahaya International is presented in Appendix B.

IN CLOSING

Opening, strengthening, and using your heart are beyond your wildest imagination and your deepest wish in living a peaceful and joyful life. It is as real as can be.

And it is so simple. All you need to do, in the end, is relax, smile, and surrender. Begin today, right now, and watch how beautifully your life changes.

May you enjoy the beauty of opening your heart for True Source every moment and share the Blessing freely with others.

14

OPEN HEART STORIES

This final chapter presents a range of stories from people hailing from many walks of life and many parts of the world who have attended the Open Heart Workshops offered by Padmacahaya International. Reading about others' experiences will hopefully help you to see how wonderful it is to finally move beyond simply knowing what your heart can do for you, to enjoying moments when you are really using your heart.

Before learning to open my heart, I didn't do much, spiritually speaking. I grew up, got married, bought a house, and had two boys. Praying and meditating were not part of my routine. Then one day I was guided to touch my heart and do Open Heart Prayer… My world hasn't been the same since!

Life took on a different meaning; it isn't the struggle it used to be. Before opening my heart, I would become so angry if a mess was made in the house, or I would grow worried about bills or get stressed out if the boys were running wild.

But since learning about the heart, I look at everything differently. When my boys are upset, instead of getting so anxious, I smile at them and do everything I can to guide and remind them about their heart. As far as messes go, messes can be cleaned up. So much stress has been eliminated since opening my heart—and whatever stress I do feel now, touching my heart and smiling for a few minutes takes care of it.

The best part, though, of having my heart opened by True Source is being so much closer—feeling how True Source Loves us so completely and relying on the Blessing to love True Source more. Praying is also so beautiful and leaves me feeling so sweet and tender…so Loved every moment. It doesn't matter what I'm doing; I know True Source is always helping us, always Loving us completely.

Crystal Sanders,
Pennsylvania

One very clear realization I had when connecting with my heart was the thought that this is so normal…so *natural*. I think that was a turning point of realizing something big.

Through the "eyes" of our heart, we can see beyond the stories that separate us from others, and instead start to witness the things that connect us. For me, it was the beginning of the relationship with unconditional Love.

Opening my heart has connected me to the mightiest force in existence: True Source. And it is *true*. It is *real*. Not an idea or a concept, but a feeling so actual and beautiful that I know—beyond any knowing my brain can ever give me—that this is the Truth, Infinite Love and Light.

Now I know I don't *have* a heart; I *am* a heart. The heart's natural role is to share with others the Love and Light that flows from True Source. What a beautiful journey it continues to be, rediscovering who I really am.

Steve Ray, Educator
Melbourne, Australia

Using my heart has changed my prayer life. I am now able to feel and experience the Love within my heart, as well as my spiritual connection to the Creator, the True Source. Praying from the heart—not just with words—allows me to feel and be grateful for the many blessings received. It helps me to surrender my problems to and rely on the Creator's Love to work on my heart and life; and helps me to realize the importance of forgiving and asking for forgiveness.

At home, being within my heart helps me smile and be more joyful when interacting with family members. It also changes doing housework, which in the past caused resentment. Caring for family members by sharing the Creator's Love is wonderful, as interactions from the heart with loved ones are now gentler, more patient, and more loving.

The way of experiencing and using the heart is the most joyful and wonderful way to live—sharing the Love with others, and loving our Creator, the True Source, more and more.

Sally Mydlowec, Executive Vice President and Dean of Academic Affairs,
Pennsylvania

Back then I was Miss Super Busy, with two cell phones and a pager, determined to succeed in the cutthroat business of real estate. I wanted to be the top agent, selling several properties each month. But at the time, making just one deal was already challenging.

Yet I was such a workaholic that I kept telling myself, "I am happy being a workaholic." I often worked until 2 a.m., on Christmas, on New Years, you name it.

Then one day, I attended a workshop given by Padmacahaya, at the insistence of my brother. In the middle of meditating, I was awestruck and thought, "Wow, this is really beautiful." At that moment, something deep within my heart was touched by the smallest drop of Love...and the most beautiful feeling in the world woke me up from my so-called reality.

Tears came running down my face for over an hour as I kept apologizing many times over. I had realized the presence of our wonderful and Loving Divine Father. I felt how Loved I was, despite all my wrongdoings. From that moment on, I vowed to live my life for True Source, because no one has ever Loved me the way True Source does. I had a purpose.

After opening my heart, I made not one deal, not two, but a whopping fourteen deals in one month—and my success has continued with me working even fewer hours and my commissions increasing. But instead of getting excited and driven to sell more, I just realize I am continually blessed.

Looking back, I can see that we are so good at fooling ourselves. I have now become so much more open-minded, patient, and caring toward others. Before I couldn't even say the word *love* without feeling uncomfortable; now I say it often everyday, with joy in my heart. I am truly grateful to True Source to have been touched and awakened.

Jennifer Lee, Real Estate Agent
Los Angeles, California

Before learning about the heart, when I prayed to True Source, it felt flat, and I was never sure if my prayers were heard. I remember how I prayed only when I had problems in my life, or because at school or at church a bunch of us were being told to pray together. Words came out of me without any feeling; I was simply reading prayer lines.

Now it is completely different: Prayers have become beautiful, and I am able to go into a deep state of connection. I feel how I am communicating with True Source, how my prayers reach up to Lovingly Listening True Source and are accepted with the beauty of Love.

Sunny Tjandrakesuma,
Melbourne, Australia

After riding the waves of life for 48 years, I started looking for the real meaning of this existence. Inadvertently, I came across the Open Heart Workshops given by Padmacahaya International, and my search ended here.

In learning about the heart, my life changed. Anger, arrogance, and other negative emotions dissipated—not because I was holding myself back from expressing them, but because they naturally started to resolve from within. As a result, my life has become more in harmony with my own family and with other people.

In the past, I sought success for its own sake in this material life. But with the heart, I realized how temporary life is; how we should enjoy it in good health, calmness, and happiness. Mere worldly success did not bring me those wonderful things.

By using my heart, wherever I am, I can avoid bad situations and be within the peace, beauty, and joy of life... while continuing to be productive and enjoying it.

Willy Iskandar, Business Owner
Jakarta, Indonesia

My life shifted after I opened my heart. The facts of my external life are still the same; but my heart attitude and my whole self have changed and are still changing.

Now that I have found my heart, I am able to stop worrying about my situations and have even become grateful for them. In my daily life, even though sometimes I am extremely busy and my job is filled with turbulence, I am more relaxed and not stressed out anymore. Surrendering to True Source, feeling the joy and peace, has also helped my biggest burden—a suppressive, desolate sadness because of loneliness—to lift more and more.

With our hearts, we are able to feel and to realize the presence, beauty, clarity, and the absoluteness of Divine Love for every being. To be allowed to experience this is the biggest joy I can imagine.

Thank You, True Source!

Angela Frenz, Contractor
Germany

Thank you, Mr. Irmansyah Effendi, for guiding me in not only getting to know myself, but to feel my true self—proving to myself beyond my knowledge the presence of the Divine Source.

Since elementary school, I have been exposed to spiritual life because I saw my parents meditate and give praise for at least 30 minutes after certain prayers. One lesson that is still etched in my memory is that there is an agreement between our spirit and our Source in the spirit world. Ever since then, I devoured spiritual books.

When I was at a boarding school, without my parents' knowledge, I studied at two different schools with two different teachings. Both taught me the use of my heart in following the teachings of my religion. This was truly the beginning of my spiritual life.

I thought my spiritual search was over then; but I was wrong. I came across books written by Mr. Irmansyah Effendi, M.Sc., about soul consciousness, Inner Heart, and the activating of the Divine Energy within. After I bought the books and read all of them, I wanted to know more and wanted to learn about channeling energy, even though I doubted that there was Divine Energy outside of my religion.

I felt I must be objective, however, and came to the conclusion that in each being there is a divine potential. Perhaps brain and thought would question this method, but the True Source's Will is the truth. I knew that with surrendering from the heart and with the Creator's Love, all human hearts will be directed to and will long for the Creator.

After I thought about the effects and the benefits that could be gained, I prayed asking for the Creator's Blessings and protection, and then attended the workshops.

Still, I thought that being able to channel Divine Energy and obtaining wonderful realizations about the Divine was the end of this. I was wrong again: Later, Mr. Effendi started the Open Heart Workshops, which I also attended. Here, my heart discovered, "This is what I have been looking for."

No words can describe the deep longing I have for True Source, in times of spiritual devotion as well as in my daily life. I am now more loving toward others and simply more patient.

Sugeng, S.Ag, Religious Teacher

I am a mother with six children and ten grandchildren. In the religious sermons that I attended, I kept hearing that praying must be accompanied with a smile and that it must come from the heart. With all the prayers that I did, I was quite content with my connection with True Source.

Then I started learning how to open and use my heart. I could feel the differences clearly before and after opening and using my heart. I became calmer, more peaceful, and more joyful. It was beautiful. I was able to get into a deep state when I prayed and I could really feel the beautiful connection every time I called out to True Source. I also started to feel the longing for True Source, and I surrendered more.

When I went on my pilgrimage again, I could definitely feel the difference between that pilgrimage and the previous one. I was filled with peace, joy, and beautiful feeling. Everything became more beautiful without anything holding my feeling back. Neither the hot weather nor the throngs of people could affect me. I was able to be there with gratitude and sincerity.

Hj Rusmala Dewy

I have never been taught how to open my heart and go into my heart in my many years as a priest and missionary. By opening my heart, I am able to feel, enjoy, and be grateful for God's everpresent Love, which is a blessing for both myself and the congregation I serve.

Fr. Ignatius Sudaryanto, CICM

I had long held the belief that truth was found only in the depth of the heart, and I reflected on this belief in two of the three books that I had written. I felt that our heart is the main key in solving all the problems we have—and with this awareness, I thought that I had used my heart in making decisions in my life. Only after attending a number of workshops given by Padmacahaya, however, did I realize I had not used my heart well at all.

After I took the workshops, I slowly began to realize the main purpose of the courses was to help participants open their hearts and improve their personal connection with True Source.

I began to feel how my heart was opening up more; it was awakened, and it started to bloom beautifully. I also began to see that our heart is very deep—beyond what we can imagine. In opening my heart, I was able to feel how True Source loves me and all His creations. My heart feels joy and peace that are beyond what I have ever experienced before.

"It's too good to be true" is what people say, and that would seem the case from the outside. Words cannot ever be enough to describe this beautiful, joyful experience, which must be experienced firsthand. As someone who thought he had used his heart, but has now realized he was wrong and is starting to learn how, I feel that the opportunity to open your heart to True Source is a priceless blessing that should be accepted with open arms.

In my role as a priest, I feel I am able to live my life and serve my congregation by using my heart. I pray more often than before, and enjoy my prayers more because I pray using my heart now. (I had not realized that my heart was often asleep when I prayed before.) And with my heart opening bigger, I also feel that I can rely on True Source's Love in doing my assignment.

For all of the Blessings I have received, I would like to express my utmost gratitude to the Most Loving True Source and to Mr. Effendi, who tirelessly teaches and guides so many people to open their hearts to love True Source more.

Thomas Tjaya

Often, I find myself sharing that before opening my heart, I sincerely believed that I was making great spiritual progress. But as I reflect back, it seems as though it was all a dream— quite unreal, quite empty and devoid of feeling. Now, as I enjoy the experience of learning to open my heart, the feeling is so wonderful, so beautiful…tears of joy arise.

I continue to honor the traditions I grew up in as a Buddhist Lama. Externally, there will always be diversity

within spirituality. I spent a whole life building bridges
between cultures and spiritual traditions, and encouraging
all I met to be more tolerant and open. But internally, at last,
I have truly found, truly experienced our unity, our common
ground. Real unity, within the realm of the heart.

Lama Thubeten Gonpo Tsering,
Illinois

By the time I was 17 years old, I had realized that loving was
the deepest, truest goal of my life: both loving True Source
and sharing love with others. So I was a bit of a know-it-all
when a friend told me about the heart—wanting to prove to
him that this was something I already understood and was
moderately proficient at doing.

Underneath, though, I was drowning. I felt desperate for
something more real. I had knowing in my philosophy and
inner wisdom, but was not able to live those things. Though
I longed to serve others, I felt blocked in being able to move
beyond concerns about my safety, ideas of happiness, and
fears. All too often, especially in public places, I closed down
inside to protect my tender feelings, and my heart and chest
felt tight. Talking myself into changing or rehearsing the
ideas and wisdom of others would last a few days but then
melt away as I fell back into habits.

I had practiced many different meditation techniques,
been guided by angels, spent weeks in silence, and changed
my life situation over and over again: single, married,
celibate monk, homeowner. Yet the rut of *ME* still held me.
How were those enlightened beings able to move out of this?
I had nearly decided that I just was not able to do it. They
had somehow been born into it or especially blessed. I was
not one of them.

After all those years of longing, it only took a few
minutes to be guided to feel my heart. The moment is fresh

for me. I was able to reach up inside and feel my connection, my very own connection with the Divine Source. The direct link between my consciousness and true Love, joy, and peace was under my nose, not above it in my head.

I could feel there was a lot of housekeeping to be done on my heart. Sadness lay around it, but a beautiful stillness I had never felt from my head radiated from within. This was not just quietness, as one feels when thoughts have calmed, but stillness, peace, and a feeling of something much more… of being Home. I was being welcomed back, step-by-step, to my true self. My life found its direction. This beautiful gift is for all of us, no matter who we are and what our situation, if we have the longing.

I actually shared the experience of the heart with one of my counseling clients, because I felt this longing from her. After a few minutes of relaxing and smiling to her heart, she exclaimed with anguish, "It's covered with black!" and a few moments later, "It's gotten so small!" Though she had not realized it before that moment, my client remembered about the heart and how beautiful it is supposed to be, blooming huge and radiating the Love and Light.

Opening your eyes to your heart reveals to all in its true form and place, clarifying everything else in your life. Nothing, absolutely nothing comes close to the feeling of it: not what the five senses can understand, no emotion, no experience, no joy from something in the world.

As I write this, it has been four years since I first learned to feel my heart. I could fill one hundred pages, one thousand pages, with one word: "gratitude."

Diana Stone, Ph.D.,
North Carolina

As a spiritual aspirant for over 30 years, and in my profession as a Ph.D. psychologist, I have experienced and taught numerous practices and approaches for enhancing well-being and spiritual growth.

In these, I used to believe I knew about being in my heart and did not realize that I was still primarily head-centered. I spent countless hours doing disciplined meditation practices and could easily experience the calm space between my thoughts. But with all those practices, I never got to experience the depth of my heart. I have come to realize that mindfulness is not the same as *heartfulness*.

If we reflect back to the most special times in which we felt so deeply touched, grateful, and connected to life— whether it was the birth of a child, a tranquil moment in nature, a peak experience, or time of spiritual communion— it was our heart that was touched. In that moment, we were connected with our heart, and that is why it felt so special and precious.

Over the entire span of a person's life, when all is said and done, and when one is about to leave this earthly plane, it is these few heartfelt experiences that give them their greatest sense of satisfaction and joy.

My happiness comes from the realization that our heart is not reserved for just a handful of special moments. We are meant to live *as a heart*, so that every moment can be special and precious, and so life is filled with abundant love and joy.

When our hearts are open, we become less and less bothered by idiosyncrasies or differences in people. Relationships begin to bring great joy; we become more accepting of our shortcomings, as well as others'; we easily forgive and share from our heart.

The quality of life improves as people realize that what used to push their buttons, or create emotional reactivity, no longer does so. And if negativity is triggered, it is significantly diminished compared to previous patterns.

They feel more sweetness and joy in their relationships, and allow the intelligence of the heart to guide their lives.

Open hearts live authentically with love, humbleness, and gratitude. And the more we are able to open our hearts, the more we are able to experience a tangible connection to the Source of Love and Light.

I am so happy that I know from the core of my heart this is something reachable and achievable for all of us. It is our birthright. I am so grateful that True Source is supporting us to fulfill this ultimate destiny.

Ed Rubenstein, Ph.D.,
North Carolina

APPENDIX A

SUPPORT CONTACT INFORMATION

Thousands of people all over the world have begun opening their hearts and meet regularly to practice, share, and enjoy. Support in your local area is just an e-mail away.

Workshops are also offered in many different countries throughout the year—regularly across the U.S., Canada, Australia, New Zealand, Germany, United Kingdom, Ireland, Singapore, Malaysia, Indonesia, and others—with local coordinators in each market.

Below is the contact information for several of our larger groups, who can put you in touch with your nearest coordinator:

Heart Sanctuary

Heart Sanctuary is a non-profit organization headquartered in Asheville, North Carolina, founded to help support and share the message that the heart is the key to a calm, joyful, healthy, and fulfilled life.

For further information:

www.heartsanctuary.org

Affiliated group based in the United Kingdom:

http://www.open-your-heart.org.uk

Lotus Centre

Lotus Centre, an organization established in Hobart, Australia, is also founded to educate the public about the heart.

For further information:

http://www.thelotuscentre.com.au

Yayasan Padmajaya

Yayasan Padmajaya was established in Indonesia in 1998 and has branches, offices, and healing clinics in many cities across the country.

For further information:

http://www.padmajaya.com

e-mail: contact@padmajaya.com

APPENDIX B

OPEN HEART WORKSHOPS (OHW) AND HEART AND SPIRITUAL QUOTIENT (HSQ) TRAINING

If you are interested in continuing the journey of opening and using your heart, a number of group programs are available from Padmacahaya International.

Following are overviews of the Open Heart Workshops and the Heart and Spiritual Quotient programs (for workplaces). For further information, local schedules, and registration, please contact your local coordinator (see Appendix A).

OPEN HEART WORKSHOPS

In this book, you have learned a natural and beautiful way to begin opening and using your heart. While still on the surface or outer part of the heart—not *within* the heart, as later workshops will instruct—the methods and basic heart exercises in this book make up the foundation for the first level of Open Heart Workshops (OHW).

Participants of these workshops meet for a full eight-hour day to practice the exercises given in this book, guided by a certified Open Heart instructor. These supportive and caring teachers have years of experience using their own hearts, and have helped hundreds of students in recognizing how to let True Source's Blessing work the best. They will not only guide you to let True Source's Blessing bring you into your heart, but help you stay there and enjoy the Blessing radiating from your heart on deeper and deeper levels. With proper guidance and more advanced and intensive heart exercises, you will be able to start using your heart maximally.

After taking or repeating the workshops (OHW Levels 1 and 2 are typically offered together on a Saturday and Sunday), participants and alumni also create support groups where they meet and practice these exercises to open and use their hearts even better.

From there, more advanced workshops are offered to help you open and use your heart the best way, and grow closer and closer to True Source. Once you are within your heart, everything becomes exponentially more beautiful.

There are six levels in the Open Heart Workshop curriculum. While each one takes you deeper, at every step you learn to:

- Let True Source's Blessing open and strengthen your heart more.
- Improve your connection to True Source, making it more beautiful.
- Surrender to True Source, as everything is about relying on True Source's Blessing.

- Achieve deeper surrendering from your heart, including surrendering your problems, burdens, and negative emotions to True Source.
- Use and enjoy your heart more in daily life.
- Maintain deeper calmness, peace, and light feeling in daily life.
- Better interact with people around you by relying on True Source's Blessing.

More specifically, following is the curriculum progression for each level of the Open Heart Workshops:

OHW Level 1

- Get to know your heart better.
- Get to know heart / feeling and brain / thoughts better.
- Strengthen your heart.
- Lessen the domination from your brain.
- Open your heart through Open Heart Meditation.
- Realize True Source's Blessing within your heart.
- Surrender more to True Source.
- Rely on True Source's Blessing within your heart in praying and living your daily life.
- Let your heart become more dominant in your daily life.

OHW Level 2

- Get truths from your heart.
- Use your heart to rely on True Source's Love in your daily life.
- Improve the feeling within your heart.

- Enjoy True Source's Love on a deeper level.
- Be more grateful while being within the Love.
- Open your heart more to True Source.
- Direct your heart even better to True Source.
- Learn to trust True Source more by surrendering our burdens and problems to True Source.

OHW Level 3

- Better realize your connection True Source.
- Cleanse and open the Divine Gate better.
- Let the Love open the chakra knots.
- Let the Love cleanse and open the main energy channel (*sushumna*).
- Let True Source's Love cleanse and improve your connection to True Source.
- Cleanse and open your heart further.
- Go into your heart.
- Pray to True Source from within your heart.
- Surrender problems and burdens from within your heart.
- Let True Source's Love work on earth and all beings on earth.
- Begin to let True Source's Love remove our heart limitations to help us move beyond our concepts and ideas of what is possible.

OHW Level 4

- Cleanse and open the Divine Gate even more.
- Let True Source's Love help for self-healing.

- Let your heart become free without being blocked, so the Love can radiate more freely and sweetly.
- Let True Source's Love bring us into the Pure Love within our heart.
- Let True Source's Love remove our limitations on a deeper level, so that the Love can work on our whole heart and our whole being.
- Surrender to True Source from within the Love in our heart.
- Interact with others from within the Love within the heart.

OHW Level 5

- Let go of the brain's and soul's influence.
- Let your Inner Heart become the director.
- Realize Real Truth using your Inner Heart.

OHW Level 6

- Realize True Source's Blessing even more.
- Share True Source's Love with others as an instrument of True Source, living your life with the realization that life is an opportunity to get closer to True Source.

HSQ® TRAINING PROGRAMS

The Heart and Spiritual Quotient® training programs are practical, hands-on workshops that help guide employees of all backgrounds toward a calmer, happier, and more effective work life. Each curriculum, which can be tailored to the specific needs/industry of practically any organization, presents a comprehensive body of theory and exercises designed to maximize each individual's implementation, usage, and growth of HSQ in their working environment.

Led by certified HSQ Instructors—each of whom has years of experience using their own hearts, as well as a solid business background—five types of HSQ training programs are offered for companies of all sizes and target specific employee groups:

1. HSQ in Leadership
2. HSQ in Management
3. HSQ in Sales & Marketing
4. HSQ in Customer Service
5. HSQ in Personal & Professional Development

HSQ in Leadership

The HSQ in Leadership training program presents a specific focus to business owners and executives on improving their perspective as leaders through the heart, as well as leveraging the heart to obtain information and guidance.

By using their hearts, business owners and leaders will be able to:

- Clearly recognize and act on the best opportunities.
- Effectively adapt themselves and the company to changing business conditions.
- Recognize personal and organizational shortcomings and willingly begin to work on them.
- Naturally choose the ideal business partners to work with and the ideal projects to take on.
- Assign the right tasks to the right managers.
- Better understand and respond to the needs of all stakeholders for the best results.

HSQ in Management

When working with more peace and clarity, managers are better able to focus on the needs of their team members, as well as approach their own responsibilities with newfound interest and enthusiasm. They are also more equipped to develop savvy managerial solutions and systems with an open heart, and can bridge the gap between driving results and promoting happiness and ease amongst the team.

Through HSQ in Management, by using their hearts, managers can:

- See opportunities to enhance business systems and processes.
- Motivate team members to do their best with sincerity.
- Naturally help to mitigate the negative emotional reactions of team members.
- Manage more calmly and communicate more effectively.
- Balance operational and personnel issues with the larger company strategic objectives.
- Achieve a smoother and more natural flow of work.
- Embrace new and existing tasks and responsibilities without feeling burdened.
- Find greater purpose and meaning in their work.

HSQ in Sales & Marketing

The real connection with the customer for a product or service often has more to do with its emotional benefits than its functional ones. The HSQ in Sales & Marketing program focuses on how to identify and tell the right story—all through using the heart.

Among the benefits, marketing and sales professionals will learn to:

- Naturally recognize the most successful sales and marketing messaging/strategies.
- Implement campaigns and utilize sales collateral more effectively.
- Market and sell products and services with heart and meaning.
- Learn to listen to customers sincerely and respond more effectively.
- Foster and further develop sincere and long-lasting relationships with new and existing clients.
- Find more purpose in what they do.

HSQ in Customer Service

Customer-facing staff are truly the frontline in the success or failure of an organization. This training curriculum was developed specifically for those working in account, sales, or service positions—learning not only to serve and smile with sincerity, but to carry this attitude through to improve their overall quality of life.

The HSQ in Customer Service training program will show representatives how to:

- Build loyalty through sincere customer service.
- Resolve customers' complaints quickly and effectively.
- Be more content with and enjoy their job on a deeper level.
- Feel lighter, calmer, and more peaceful when interacting with customers.

- Smile from the heart sincerely to customers in both face-to-face interactions and on-the-phone conversations.
- Receive a more open, positive reaction from customers who see the smile on their faces or hear the smile in their voices.
- Become mentally, physically, and emotionally healthier.

HSQ in Personal & Professional Development

Companies can leverage the HSQ in Personal & Professional Development training program as a standalone group event, or implement it as a strategic add-on to an existing company activity, offsite, or retreat to:

- Turn brainstorming sessions into "heart storming" sessions, where group dynamics become more collaborative and new solutions flow more naturally.
- Add a new dimension to a company's team-building and incentive program activities (e.g., using HSQ to play better golf).
- Boost staff morale and reduce turnover.
- Enhance any ongoing staff wellness program.
- Help staff to live in the present moment with a more grateful attitude toward life in general.

Other Ulysses Press Mind/Body Titles

1325 Buddhist Ways to Be Happy
Barbara Ann Kipfer, $13.95
This book looks at everyday situations and provides the Buddha's and other Buddhist teachers' guidance for navigating them in a cheerful, positive way. The sayings in this book allow readers of any faith (or no faith) to explore the Buddha's ideas and relate them to their own personal quest for happiness.

863 Buddhist Ways to Conquer Life's Little Challenges
Barbara Ann Kipfer, $14.95
Whether the reader is a practicing Buddhist or just seeking a little peace to the daily grind, the crystal-clear lessons in this book allow anyone to establish a calming meditative rhythm every day.

How Meditation Heals: Scientific Evidence and Practical Applications
2nd edition, Eric Harrison, $14.95
In straightforward, practical terms, How Meditation Heals reveals how and why meditation improves the natural functioning of the human body.

Flip the Switch: 40 Anytime, Anywhere Meditations in 5 Minutes or Less
Eric Harrison, $10.95
Specially designed meditations that fit any situation: idling at a red light, waiting for a computer to restart, or standing in line at the grocery store.

Teach Yourself to Meditate in 10 Simple Lessons:
Discover Relaxation and Clarity of Mind in Just
Minutes a Day
Eric Harrison, $13.95
Ideal for beginning students, this book guides the reader through a
series of core meditations that the author has carefully honed over
the years while personally guiding his students.

The 7 Healing Chakras: Unlocking Your Body's
Energy Centers
Dr. Brenda Davies, $14.95
Explores the essence of chakras, vortices of energy that connect the
physical body with the spiritual.

The 7 Healing Chakras Workbook: Exercises for
Unlocking Your Body's Energy Centers
Dr. Brenda Davies, $16.95
Filled with step-by-step guided activities, this workbook offers a
voyage of self-discovery that allows you to achieve your full poten-
tial and improve virtually every aspect of your life.

To order these books call 800-377-2542 or 510-601-8307, e-mail
ulysses@ulyssespress.com, or write to Ulysses Press, P.O. Box
3440, Berkeley, CA 94703. All retail orders are shipped free of
charge. California residents must include sales tax. Allow two
to three weeks for delivery.

ABOUT THE AUTHOR

Irmansyah ("Irman") Effendi, M.Sc., has been teaching about the heart for more than a decade, helping hundreds of thousands of people through his workshops, healing clinics, nonprofits, and business training programs. Beginning his career in computer science—earning a master's degree in artificial intelligence at age twenty-one—Irman began to realize about the beauty and meaning of the heart through intensive spiritual practice and study. Since 1998, he has devoted his life to helping people all around the world open and enjoy using their hearts, and has written more than twelve books on the subject. (This is his first major English-language release).

Originally from Indonesia, Irman now makes his home in Perth, Australia.